Enter the New Negroes

Enter the New Negroes

Images of Race in American Culture

Martha Jane Nadell

Harvard University Press
Cambridge, Massachusetts, and London, England   2004

Excerpts from Langston Hughes, *One-Way Ticket,* are from
Selected Poems of Langston Hughes, copyright © 1927 by Alfred
Knopf, Inc., and renewed 1955 by Langston Hughes. Used by
permission of Alfred A. Knopf, a division of Random House, Inc.,
and by permission of Harold Ober Associates.

Library of Congress Cataloging-in-Publication Data

Nadell, Martha Jane.
Enter the new Negroes : images of race in American culture /
Martha Jane Nadell.
p.   cm.
Includes index.
ISBN 0-674-01511-8 (alk. paper)
1. African Americans in popular culture.   2. African Americans in
literature.   3. African Americans—Intellectual life—20th century.
4. Harlem Renaissance.   5. Popular culture—United States—
History—20th century.   6. American literature—20th century—
History and criticism.   I. Title.

E185.6.N165   2004
305.896′073—dc22   2004052365

Designed by Gwen Nefsky Frankfeldt

For my parents

Acknowledgments

Y FIRST DEBT is to Werner Sollors, whose passion for and depth of knowledge have long been an inspiration to me. Over the years, he has become my ideal reader and a valuable and constant friend. Henry Louis Gates Jr. has been exceptionally supportive and encouraging. His readings made my work infinitely better. Cornel West has been a friend, mentor, and intellectual partner who offered support, kindness, and generosity as I worked on this manuscript.

I would like to thank the following friends and colleagues: Anthony Appiah, Maria Ascher, Mia Bay, Emily Bernard, Adam Biggs, Suzanne Blier, Adam Bradley, Alide Cagidemetrio, Frank Cooper, Karen Dalton, Nick Dames, Miriam Deutsch, Neal Dolan, Charatini Douvaldzi, Ingrid Geerken, Farah Jasmine Griffin, Louise Hainline, Mary Hamer, Jonathan Hexner, Monica Hexner, Evelyn Brooks Higginbotham, Nathan Huggins, the Jewett family, Barbara Karasinski, Peter Lurie, Stephen Marshall, Christine McFadden, Jeff Melnick, Inge Morath, Richard Newman, Anita Patterson, Miranda Pyne, Renate Reiss, Maren Stange, Jeffrey Stewart, Ellen Tremper, Helen Vendler, Lynn Weiss, Richard Wendorf, Diana Williams, Andre Willis, Tom Wirth, and my numerous new colleagues at Brooklyn College. Special thanks to Tom Hexner and Amy King, and to Kathleen McDermott, whose benevolent but firm insistence got me through crucial stages of the writing process.

I would like to thank all of those unsuspecting students on whom I tried out my ideas over the years. These include Gretchen Brion-Miesels,

Omiyinka Doris, Felicia Gordon, Kamil Redmomd, Aparna Sridhar, and the students in my freshman seminars: Uchechi Acholonu, Matt Amato, Joy Cooper, Rini Fonseca-Sabune, Ronni Gaillard, Sophie Gonick, Megumi Gordon, Jillion Harris, Damon King, Sonia Kpaduwa, Onyi Offor, Stephanie Paiz, Stella Safo, Tina Tanhehco, Catherine Tung, and Wordna Warren. Special thanks go to Sarah Lewis, whose research assistance, critical eye, and good humor improved the quality of my work.

Thanks to Ami Parekh, Darshani Kahanda, and Olga Kirsanova of the Brooklyn College Faculty Training and Development Lab, and especially to Martha Kennedy of the Prints and Photographs Division of the Library of Congress. I greatly appreciate the support of Brooklyn College. I would not have been able to complete this project without support from the Mark DeWolfe Howe Fund, the History of American Civilization Summer Awards, and the Swann Foundation Fellowship for Cartoon and Caricature at the Library of Congress.

I gratefully acknowledge the following for permission to reprint images and use excerpts from unpublished letters: the Poetry and Rare Books Collection, State University of New York at Buffalo; Black Classic Press; the Moorland-Spingarn Room, Howard University; the Helen Hall Kellogg estate; Renate Reiss; the library at Universidad de las Americas; the National Urban League; the Fisk University Art Galleries; the National Portrait Gallery; the Wolfsonian–Florida International University; the Schomburg Center for Research in Black Culture; Fire Press; Tom Wirth; HarperCollins Publishers; Alfred A. Knopf, Inc.; the Beinecke Library at Yale University; the Houghton Library at Harvard University; the Artists' Rights Society; the Langston Hughes Estate; Harold Ober Associates, Inc.; and Gwendolyn Knight Lawrence.

A number of individuals accompanied me through the difficult process of completing this work. Anne Hallward and Susan Siroty enabled me to muster the necessary courage and stamina, while Lorca and Mistral were my constant companions. Toby and Caleb brought me nothing but joy. I am lucky to have as a sister-in-law a peer and a best friend: Brooke Jewett Nadell listened, read, edited, and counseled. My brothers, Bernhardt and Teddy, have been models of intellectual curiosity and hard work. And I owe the greatest thanks to Humberto Mata, whose love and care I have enjoyed for many years.

I dedicate this book to my parents: the late Raymond Nadell, a great analyst and astute reader of people, and Shari Nadell, a remarkable artist and gifted intellectual.

Contents

Illustrations

Enter the New Negroes

Introduction

To rid ourselves of this damaging distortion of art values by color-line, we shall have to draw the culture-line sharply and without compromise.

—Alain Locke, "To Certain of Our Philistines"

Harlem in the 1920s was a remarkable place. It was the scene of great social upheaval and transformation. According to some critics of the time, it represented the maturation of African Americans into their modern, urban incarnation. Home to an incredibly diverse black population that cut across social strata and nationalities, Harlem embraced old and new inhabitants: migrants, immigrants, and native New Yorkers. The anonymous farm worker coming to Harlem from the South and the recognizable A'Lelia Walker (daughter of America's first black female millionaire), churchgoers and nightclubbers, poets and laborers—all mingled on the wide avenues and narrow streets of northern Manhattan. This assortment of individuals—many of whom had arrived in Harlem during the Great Migration of African Americans from the rural South to the urban North and Midwest beginning in the 1890s, and others of whom had come from the West Indies or Africa—provided rich material for the writers, artists, and intellectuals who gathered in Harlem.

African American writer Eric Walrond, who would publish the novel *Tropic Death* in 1926, wrote about elements of this population in *Vanity Fair* in 1924:

> The effortless New York public, revolving always with the fairest wind, has recently discovered a new brand of Negro entertainer. Not the old type, of course. The lullaby-singer has gone. Also the plantation darky. And, out of the welter of sentimentality which the old types created, the Negro now emerges as an individual, an individual as brisk and as actual as your own next-door neighbor. He no longer has to be either a Pullman car porter, or

over-fond of watermelon, in order to be a successful type on our stage. He is a personality, always, and frequently an artist.[1]

The typology of the minstrel, the Pullman car porter, and the watermelon eater is here banished and recognized as defunct. In its place, Walrond proclaims, are stage personalities rather than stereotypical watermelon eaters, artists instead of train porters, and, most important, individuals and not "old types." The sentiment encapsulated in this *Vanity Fair* piece was pervasive among Harlem critics, writers, and artists. A sense of newness, possibility, and individuality ran through the remarkable amount of literary and visual work produced at that time.

Those who watched from outside the borders of this northern Manhattan community also saw something momentous and new emerging out of the Great Migration. For Paul Kellogg, the development of this vibrant urban area was the inspiration for a special number of the magazine he edited, the *Survey Graphic,* a monthly devoted to social work: "The northward migration of the southern Negroes, of course, has something of this epic quality to it and we hit upon the idea of taking Harlem as the stage in order to visualize it—Harlem, which with its southern and West Indian influx has become, I suppose, the greatest Negro community in the world. More than that, there has been a flaring out of cultural life there. The Negro is expressing himself in new ways."[2] The sense that there was in Harlem something unusual, noteworthy, and new was widespread; the consciousness engendered fresh meanings for an old nomenclature.[3] The expressive Negroes of 1920s Harlem—writers, artists, intellectuals, and performers—became known as "New Negroes." And the "flaring out of cultural life," the upsurge in literary and artistic productions, led the era to be dubbed the Harlem Renaissance.

Those years saw an unprecedented amount of analysis and criticism of the time itself, resulting in part from the concentration of so many of these writers, artists, and intellectuals living, at times in close quarters, in northern Manhattan. Much of the self-reflexive inquiry negotiated this moment of great social upheaval. Given a past of slavery and Jim Crow in the South, and outmoded stereotypes that fixed African Americans in unrealistic categories, how was this newly urban and lately modern people to imagine itself, its present, and its future? Questions posed by these Harlemites revolved around the nature of African American identity and around representations about and by African Americans: What was black identity in that era and place of great social change? Who were the "New Negroes"? Who should produce art, of any sort, about these "New Negroes"? Should only one "type" of African American serve as the exemplar of all African Americans, or should artists embrace everyone, from prostitutes to the respectable men of the middle class?

Critics debated issues such as whether the Negro population demanded journalistic or realistic approaches. Some asked if Harlem needed sociological or historical surveys of the patterns of its communities, or fictional or dramatic accounts of the individuals who populated it. Others considered the possibility that the New Negro was best served by Modernist-inflected art and literature—abstract, experimental, self-conscious forms that could embrace both the modernity of the population and the concomitant developments in the larger American literary and visual fields. For almost all critics, one central question was how to attack stereotypes while accounting for the growth of this newly urban African American population.

Other questions revolved around how representation should be disseminated. Was it better to produce novels or magazines, paintings or mass-produced illustrations? Should publishers actively encourage or discourage certain kinds of depictions or vehicles of expression? Should publications be black-produced and black-directed, or was there room for white writers, artists, publishers, editors, and their magazines in the circle of African American expression?

Debates about these questions surfaced in print throughout the 1920s. Poet Langston Hughes and critic George Schuyler argued in the pages of the *Nation* about what constituted African American art, publishing "The Negro Artist and the Racial Mountain" and "The Negro-Art Hokum," respectively. In 1926 the foremost African American intellectual of the twentieth century, W. E. B. Du Bois, sponsored a symposium in the *Crisis,* the magazine affiliated with the National Association of the Advancement of Colored People. Entitled "The Negro in Art: How Shall He Be Portrayed?" the symposium was a forum for ideas about appropriate representations of African Americans and about the responsibilities of authors, artists, and publishers in producing and disseminating those representations.

As the Harlem Renaissance declined in the early 1930s, the left-wing magazine *New Masses* framed questions about racial representation in a new way, heralding a shift in critical thought on representations of African American life in the 1930s and 1940s. In May 1930, the magazine published a pair of images whose subject was two competing versions of "the Negro"; one was "the white bourgeois version" and the other "as the white worker knows him." A "white bourgeois" couple—a woman wearing a fashionable hat and holding a cigarette holder and a man in jacket and tie—are in the foreground of one of the line drawings (Figure 1). Behind the couple are a variety of images of African Americans, all seemingly

Figure 1. William Siegel, *The White Bourgeois Version of the Negro*. Illustration for New Masses, May 1930. Courtesy of the Poetry and Rare Books Collection, University Libraries, State University of New York at Buffalo.

Figure 2. William Siegel, *The Negro as the White Worker Knows Him.* Illustration for *New Masses*, May 1930. Courtesy of the Poetry and Rare Books Collection, University Libraries, State University of New York at Buffalo.

stereotypes: a pair of black men gamble, while a nearly nude woman dances near a presumably jazz-playing saxophonist as a man leers at her. This is "Harlem," according to a word scrawled near these figures. Other figures round out the image: two Africans, one in a mask and the other wearing an earring and face paint, beat a drum on which is written "hoo doo." The "cotton fields" occupy the upper right-hand corner, where Southern blacks wearing kerchiefs eat watermelon and worship.[4]

Another couple, identified as white workers, occupy the foreground of the other drawing (Figure 2). Behind them are dignified black workers with gentle faces who read, cook, dig, hoe, and carry burdens. Images of migrants walking past apartment buildings and factories allude to the Great Migration, while a mob surrounding a burning man tied to a tree refers to the lynchings that took place in the South.

In many respects, these images are a challenge to the Harlem Renaissance. They suggest that the movement—and the whites who believed in it—trafficked in notions of black exoticism, primitivism, and naïve Southern black religiosity. A better representation, the images imply, would revolve around the dignity of work and education in the face of the brutal realities of Southern lynching, and attention to the connections between race and class would provide a greater insight into African American life than the stereotypes associated with Harlem and the South.

If the debates about the representation of African Americans were an explicit subject for criticism in the 1920s, '30s, and '40s, they were an equally important concern—though often an implicit one—for the many novels, anthologies, collections of poetry, and histories that were published during those decades. Artists worked on visualizing the human figure without caricature in their book illustrations, while writers attempted to force language beyond the dialect that had dominated in the nineteenth century or took vernacular language into new directions, thereby challenging myriad assumptions about African American characteristics. In 1927, the painter Aaron Douglas used black-and-white contrast and geometric shapes to render the lead character of Eugene O'Neill's play *The Emperor Jones,* portrayed by Paul Robeson, who had, a few years earlier, been photographed in minstrel pants and a fright wig. The writer Jean Toomer turned the modernist movement known as Imagism toward a struggle with racial identity in the 1920s.[5] In the 1930s, the poet and critic Sterling Brown reconceived the dialect of Paul Laurence Dunbar's turn-of-the-century poetry. And in the 1940s, Richard Wright, in his novel *Native Son,* introduced Bigger Thomas to portray black urban life with a unique blend of modernist and naturalist writing.

The following discussion looks at a little-studied subset of those literary works that meditated on the relationship between race and representation. It examines how a number of African American works employed visual images along with text to speculate on the nature of African American identity, communities, and history.

Despite the general decline in the publication of illustrated material in American arts and letters during the first half of the twentieth century, many African American writers of that era published works that contained illustrations or other forms of visual material. I call these works "interartistic," a term I borrow from Wendy Steiner and by which I mean publications that concretely mix word and image and foreground the relationship between the two media.[6] This book explores the surprising prevalence and importance of what scholar Marcus Woods calls "quoted imagery" (or "reproduced imagery") in African American print culture from the 1920s to the 1940s.

We will see that the image became an integral part of African American literary texts as writers and artists wrestled with the changes wrought by the Great Migration, the growing urbanism of the black population, the continued vibrancy of folk life, and the relationship between class and race. In various ways, images filled out literary efforts to confront the nature of African America during the first half of the twentieth century, providing multiple viewpoints on the complexities of the era.

At LEAST since HORACE, critics have formulated theories about the similarities and dissimilarities between the "sister arts" of literature and visual art. They have compared independent examples of the two forms in an effort to formulate ideas about the *Zeitgeist* of an era or attempted to create theories about the differences and similarities of the two media. In the chapters that follow, I will not attempt to provide a comprehensive overview of these discussions or to formulate a unified theory of image and text relations. Rather, I will employ the approaches of critics most useful for the purposes of my discussion of African American interartistic work.

W. J. T. Mitchell's work is a rich resource—a complex and nuanced meditation on the relation between word and image and on scholarship about that relation. It is helpful in discussions of African American interartistic work on three counts. First, Mitchell argues that the most productive arenas for discussion of the word/image problem are the concrete forms in which "visual-verbal relationships are unavoidable—such as films, plays, newspapers, cartoon strips, illustrated books." Second, he emphasizes the contingency and heterogeneity of the relations between image and text. He is skeptical of constructing a cohesive theory of word-and-image relations, preferring instead to foreground the multiplicity of possible interactions and of possible interpretations. He thus imagines the field as a "problem" of fluid and makeshift boundaries between media, across which occur "mutual migration, cultural exchange, and other forms of intercourse." Third, he sees surfacing within the word/image problem and discussions of it "questions of power, value, and human interest." Discussions of semiotic difference, he writes, are frequently connected to ideas of social difference.[7]

My work follows Mitchell in that it insists on exploring the complexity and variability of word/image relations within works that mix the two media on the material level. Accordingly, I use the term "interartistic" to describe works that comprise—and hence make problematic, as Mitchell would argue—the visual and the textual. I discuss magazines that employ photographs, portraits, and sketches to further their editorial aims, collections of poetry that include illustrations of specific poems, nonfiction works in which image and text at times conflict, and collaborations in which writers and artists respond to each other's visions. Interartistic works thus include a wide array of material that can follow the conventions of their forms (say, of subordinating the visual to the literary in illustrated novels) or exhibit complicated and unexpected intersections between the two media (such as James Agee and Walker Evans' *Let Us Now Praise Famous Men,* which, as Mitchell writes, resists an expected "suturing of the word and image").[8]

In the mid-1990s, a number of scholars of African American studies came together to develop a "common mode of inquiry for the study of black artistic expression."[9] Rightly recognizing the "interdisciplinary nature of much black art," they wanted to develop a "common vocabulary" to discuss the cross-fertilization in music, literature, art, and other forms of black creative expression.[10] Yet this goal proved elusive, and while the scholars produced readings of African American dance, poetry, art, and other forms (published in the journal *Lenox Avenue*), they did not define a single method of inquiry for this field. Mitchell again is helpful here, since he remains unconvinced that there is a "stable theoretical foundation for regulating comparative studies of words and images." Instead, he asks us to consider "the whole ensemble of *relations* between media." He writes, "Difference is just as important as similarity, antagonism as crucial as collaboration, dissonance and division of labor as interesting as harmony and blending of function."[11] Thus, rather than attempt to fix a single manner in which word and image interact in African American print culture, I consider the relations between the two media as they emerge in specific works, often in idiosyncratic ways.

Mitchell and the scholars affiliated with *Lenox Avenue* agree on the importance of attending to social and cultural context in the word-and-image field. *Lenox Avenue* concentrates on what its editors call the "integrative" nature of African American cultural production. I will discuss the word/image problem in interartistic texts in light of the circumstances of their production and in the context of debates central to the African American population.

THIS BOOK THUS EXAMINES a number of works in which the problem of word and image demands attention, ranging from Alain Locke's anthology *The New Negro: An Interpretation* (1925) to Langston Hughes and Jacob Lawrence's illustrated volume of poetry *One Way Ticket* (1949). Yet this book also approaches another, equally important issue. It considers how literary and visual images of race changed from the 1920s, when the Harlem Renaissance was in full swing, through the 1930s and 1940s, the age of the Depression and World War II. How did the modernist experimentations in envisioning the New Negro, through visual images that were simultaneously abstract and figurative, give way to sketches that played with the idea of anthropological realism? How did the self-consciously avant-garde literary work of the younger generation of the Harlem Renaissance—short stories, poems, and articles that were experimental in form and daring in content—shift to a Marxist-inflected historical account of the Great Migration and interracial relations in the 1940s? Were Harlem Renaissance writers and artists responding in literary and visual forms to the growing modernity of the African American population and the nation in general—changes in demographics, the built environment, transportation, and technology? Were later writers and artists concerned with a different set of issues—ideas of disappearing folklife, the poverty wrought by the Great Depression, the experience of African American soldiers returning to a segregated society? Word and image, in each work that this book examines, tell part of the story of how images of race shifted during the first half of the twentieth century in response to earlier images and to cultural shifts.

chapter one

Exit the Old Negro

In December 1924, *Vanity Fair* proclaimed the arrival of the "New Negro." With striking images by caricaturist cum anthropologist Miguel Covarrubias and captions by the West Indian essayist Eric Walrond, the magazine named the avatar of a new era in a two-page spread entitled "Enter the New Negro, a Distinctive Type Recently Created by the Coloured Cabaret Belt in New York." A few months later, in March 1925, Alain Locke, a philosopher educated at Harvard and Oxford and, some would argue, the godfather of the Harlem Renaissance, echoed these sentiments in an essay published in a special issue of the *Survey Graphic,* a monthly magazine of social work. In "Enter the New Negro," he heralded the latest arrival on the New York scene, a figure emerging from the shift in the African American population from rural to urban, from South to North, and, he contended, from premodern to modern.[1]

The subtitle of the 1924 *Vanity Fair* piece was "Exit the Coloured Crooner of Lullabys, the Cotton-Picker, the Mammy Singer and the Darky Banjo-Player." In "Enter the New Negro," Locke likewise bid goodbye to "aunties," "uncles," "mammies," "Uncle Tom," and "Sambo"—actors in a "popular melodrama" that had "played itself out." It was time, Locke argued, "to scrap the fictions, garret the bogeys and settle down to a realistic facing of facts."[2]

If a central part of the invention of the New Negro was the creation of an appropriate and useful racial aesthetic for the era, another equally important part was the articulation of an Old Negro, who was not quite invented but rather culled from a wide variety of nineteenth-century literary and visual images of African Americans. Hence, Walrond and Locke juxtaposed their images of urban, artistic, modern African Americans with a set of nineteenth-century images—the mammy, the darky banjo-player, Uncle Tom, and others. These Old and New Negroes formed an unstable yet productive dialectic that engendered ideas about race, realism, and stereotype—ideas that would inform the work of writers and artists for generations to come.

Scholars Henry Louis Gates Jr. and Eric Sundquist point to the fluidity of the term "New Negro," a fluidity that in turn affects its partner, the term "Old Negro."[3] In the decade before "New Negro" came to be associated with the cultural agenda of the Harlem Renaissance, the term suggested a radical political orientation. Consider, for example, a cartoon published in the *Messenger* in 1919, a mere six years before Locke published his anthology of literature and art, *The New Negro: An Interpretation*. The image depicts the Old/New dichotomy in terms of black leadership. The New Negroes are radicals who brandish guns to defend themselves against mob violence. W. E. B. Du Bois and Booker T. Washington stand for the "old crowd Negro," whose sentiments—"Close ranks. Let us forget our grievances" and "Be modest and unassuming"—the radical magazine rejected.[4] Yet Du Bois and Washington, Old Negroes in 1919, had been new a mere nineteen years before, when Washington had published *A New Negro for a New Century,* a collection of essays and photographs depicting the "the Upward Struggles of the Negro Race."[5] As Gates writes, Washington's anthology imagined a new "Public Negro Self" in contrast to the "Negro of thirty years ago."[6] Its Old Negro consisted of "stereotypes scattered throughout plantation fictions, blackface minstrelsy, vaudeville, racist pseudo-science, and vulgar Darwinism."[7]

Writing the Old Negro

By 1925, the Old/New Negro dichotomy had adopted the terms of the cultural orientation of the Harlem Renaissance. Locke and other critics juxtaposed the work of up-and-coming Harlem Renaissance writers—such as Claude McKay, Langston Hughes, Jean Toomer and other members of the "Younger Generation"—with earlier representations of African Americans in American literature and art.[8] This work had been produced predominantly by non–African Americans rather than by earlier African American writers, such as Paul Laurence Dunbar, Charles Chesnutt, Washington, and Du Bois.[9] William Stanley Braithwaite (in "The Negro in Literature," *Crisis,* 1924; revised for Locke's 1925 anthology), Benjamin Brawley (in "The Negro in American Fiction," *Dial,* 1919), Locke (in "American Literary Tradition and the Negro," *Modern Quarterly,* 1926), and others looked at the failings of literature of the past as a way of conveying the creativity, the originality, and especially the honesty and faithfulness of contemporary work. The Old Negro existed in literature that failed to do justice to, as Braithwaite put it, "the most precious mass of raw material for literature."[10] He was a fictitious slave devoted to his master in the South created by Harriet Beecher Stowe, or a former slave who longed for the plantations imagined by Joel Chandler Harris and Thomas Nelson Page in the years after Reconstruction. He was a lascivious, aggressive pretender to political power or a beast intent on interracial rape in the Reconstruction of Thomas Dixon. He was an Uncle Tom or a Sambo. His female counterpart was a Mammy or a Jezebel. All of these were specious myths of African American identity promulgated by white writers, myths that the New Negroes would combat through their contemporary work.

Although they disagreed about the details, critics wrote literary histories, of a sort. They organized these representations of African Americans in American literature into distinct periods, and, almost to a man, condemned the same set of white writers for perpetuating particularly troubling images of African Americans.[11]

Despite the publication and popularity of other novels of the era, Harriet Beecher Stowe's 1852 abolitionist text *Uncle Tom's Cabin, or Life Among the Lowly* occupied a central position for Braithwaite, Brawley, Locke, and others.[12] They recognized the extraordinary influence of Stowe's book not only for its representations of African America and its enormous popularity (it had gone through dozens of printings by the Harlem Renaissance), but also for its centrality within American racial discourse.

The novel offers a set of characters that became, as Locke put it, "stock figures."[13] Topsy is an irrepressible imp, and Aunt Chloe a nurturing Mammy figure. Uncle Tom is a pious, devout, loving servant with a childlike faith in Jesus and his master. Yet it wasn't simply Uncle Tom qua character that bothered Braithwaite and others. It was the manner in which he became a fixture in America's racial imagination. Braithwaite spoke of the way Uncle Tom moved from the text to dominate American ideas about race in the mid- to late nineteenth century:

Controversy and moral appeal gave us *Uncle Tom's Cabin,*—the first conspicuous example of the Negro as a subject for literary treatment. Published in

1852, it dominated in mood and attitude the American literature of a whole generation; until the body of Reconstruction literature with its quite different attitude came into vogue. Here was sentimentalized sympathy for a downtrodden race, but one in which was projected a character, in Uncle Tom himself, which has been unequalled in its hold upon the popular imagination to this day.[14]

Braithwaite could have extended his sense of the ubiquity of Uncle Tom well into the twentieth century and across the Atlantic. Stowe's work was the source of a veritable industry within popular culture. In the mid-nineteenth century, Uncle Tom emerged onstage and would later make appearances in film and cartoons. His face graced playing cards, sheet music, and even Italian ceramics.[15] In short, Uncle Tom became an omnipresent figure within the performance, visual, and material cultures of the nineteenth and twentieth centuries.

In the literary histories written by Harlem Renaissance and later critics, the Plantation School of the postbellum era followed Stowe. This period was dominated, as Brawley writes, by "four exponents of Southern life": Joel Chandler Harris, George Washington Cable, Thomas Nelson Page, and Thomas Dixon. All were literary heirs to Stowe—white authors of problematic African American characters.[16]

For Harlem Renaissance critics, these writers presented a particular challenge, for they imagined an Old/New Negro dichotomy that celebrated an imagined docile slave and condemned a fictitious postbellum Negro, who was socially and sexually aggressive. The Old Negro was an "old darky" or "old-time darky"; the "new-issue nigger" was the "post-Reconstruction Negro, . . . predisposed to loafing, stealing, and effrontery," as Eric Sundquist writes.[17]

Harris' "old darky" was Uncle Remus, the subject of a multivolume series of short stories, beginning in 1881 with the publication of *Uncle Remus: His Songs and Sayings*. Uncle Remus was a former slave who recounted African American folktales in dialect to the grandson and (by the conclusion of the series) to the great-grandson of his former master. The folktales—about Brer Rabbit, Brer Duck, and others—are framed by Uncle Remus' reflections, which exhibit nostalgia for the slave past and often a bemused contempt for the post-Reconstruction present.

Cable was most widely known for his novels of Creole New Orleans. His 1881 novel *The Grandissimes* addressed race mixing and caste stratification within the Creole population around the time of the 1803 Louisiana Purchase and subtly commented on Reconstruction Louisiana. It considered a range of characters, including two half-brothers, both named

Honoré Grandissime, but one white and socially prominent and the other racially mixed and an outcast. Cable also included a character named Bras-Coupé, an African slave who is described as "an animal that could not be whipped."[18]

Page's "old-time darkies" included characters like Sam, who appears in "Marse Chan," a short story collected in the volume entitled *In Ole Virginia* (1887). The stories are shot through with nostalgia for an imaginary and idyllic Southern past, when masters were benevolent and slaves devoted. Sam is a former slave who looks back fondly on his plantation days and on his master, whom he adored: "Dem wuz good ole times, marster—de bes' Sam ever see! Dey wuz, in fac'! Niggers didn' hed nothin' 't all to do—jes' hed to 'ten' to de feedin' an' cleanin' de hosses, an' doin' what de marster tell 'em to do; an' when dey wuz sick, dey had things sont 'em out de house, an' de same doctor come to see 'em whar 'ten' to de white folks when dey wuz po'ly. Dyar warn' no trouble nor nothin'."[19] Page's work presents elements typical of some of the writing of the Plantation School. It depicts a tranquil antebellum era, described in dialect by a former slave. The imagined Southern past was a happy time when slaves gladly did the bidding of their masters, and the masters, in turn, took good care of their slaves.

Page also published a novel entitled *Red Rock* (1902). This text is representative of another strain in the Plantation School: the Reconstruction novel. *Red Rock* focuses on the racial and sectional strains of the period immediately following the Civil War. The villains include carpetbaggers with names like Jonadab Leech, and the Ku Klux Klan is organized to defend the Southern way of life. In this Reconstruction world, former slaves remain loyal to their masters and their antebellum way of life, even refusing wages offered to them for work. One former slave remarks, "Ef jest my *ole master* could come back. He'd know I didn' do it for no wages."[20] Yet dangerous black men, who threaten genteel white women, appear in the text. Moses, for example, is described as "reptile," a "species of worm," an "impudent dog," and a "wild beast" who tears at the skirt of a white woman.[21]

Thomas Dixon also imagined a bestial nature for African Americans. His Klan trilogy comprised *The Leopard's Spots* (1902), *The Clansmen* (1905; the inspiration for D. W. Griffith's 1915 film *Birth of a Nation*), and *The Traitor* (1907). While there is an occasional loyal former slave in *The Leopard's Spots* (which is subtitled *A Romance of the White Man's Burden, 1865–1900*), African Americans are generally painted as an imminent, uncontrollable danger: "In every one of these soldiers' hearts, and over all the earth, hung the shadow of the freed Negro, transformed by the exigency of war from a Chattel, to be bought and sold, into a possible Beast to be feared and guarded. Around this dusky figure every white man's soul was keeping its grim vigil."[22] Former slaves are lazy, aggressive, and violent. They are greedy and prone to drunkenness, rape, and murder. Their aim is to create a black nation in the South:

> We will drive the white man out of this country. That is the purpose of our friends at Washington. If white men want to live in the South they can become our servants. If they don't like their job they can move to a more congenial climate. You have Congree on your side, backed by a million bayonets. There is no President. The Supreme Court is chained. In San Domingo no white man is allowed to vote, hold office or hold a foot of land. We will make this mighty South a more glorious San Domingo.[23]

The threat of this "new-issue nigger" is political, social, and sexual. Marauding bands of black soldiers attack virtuous young white women, who subsequently die, while corrupt politicians attempt to overturn the racial hierarchy of the South.

Critics did not condemn these Plantation School writers with equal vigor. Braithwaite, for example, relished the way Harris used language: there was "something approaching true portraiture" in Harris' folktales. Harris was, in his opinion, a "providentially provided amanuensis for preserving the folk tales and legends" for an illiterate race.[24] Braithwaite clearly had in mind Harris' folktales, rather than the framing device in which the nostalgia for the imagined antebellum time and the anxiety about the post-Reconstruction era surface. Uncle Remus' language seems genuine, and Braithwaite sees Harris as recording the authentic cadences and vocabulary of the black vernacular.

Brawley, who agreed that Harris was somehow more benign than other writers, gave the deep and troubling racism in Page and Dixon's work special attention:

> But more serious is the tone when we come to Thomas Nelson Page and Thomas Dixon. We might tarry for a few minutes with Mr. Page to listen to more such tales as those of Uncle Remus; but we must turn to living issues. Times have changed. The grandson of Uncle Remus does not feel that he must stand with his hat in his hand when he is in our presence, and he even presumes to help us in the running of our government. This will never do; so in *Red Rock* and *The Leopard's Spots* it must be shown that he should have never been allowed to vote anyway, and those honorable gentlemen in the Congress of the United States in the year 1865 did not know at all what they were about. Though we are given the characters and setting of a novel, the

real business is to show that the Negro has been the "sentimental pet" of the nation all too long. By all means let us have an innocent white girl, a burly Negro, and a burning at the stake, or the story would be incomplete.[25]

Brawley refers specifically to the manner in which the writers preyed on white anxiety about black sexual aggression and investment in white female innocence, a deadly combination in the text and in the Jim Crow era in which it was written.

Writers of the 1910s and later, such as Octavus Roy Cohen and Haldane Macfall, were no better in the minds of critics. Cohen wrote a series of short stories about "Birmingham's Darktown." They featured characters with names like Orifice R. Latimer, J. Caesar Clump, and Iodinah Jones. Florian Slappey, a bumbling black detective, was especially popular, appearing regularly in stories published in the *Saturday Evening Post*.[26] Macfall was, according to critic Emmett Scott, "a sort of British Octavus Roy Cohen." Scott described Macfall's novel *The Wooings of Jezebel Pettyfer*, a tale about black Barbados, as follows: "The tone of the whole novel is one of sustained contempt, almost hatred, for Negroes. . . . About midway through the book, Macfall abandons such labored attempts at humor, puts aside all sympathy for his characters, and begins to show himself a genuine Negro-hater. From this point on all Negro women are 'slipshod Negresses,' or 'slattern gossips,' or something equally offensive. Negro men are ape-like. They do not think—ideas 'penetrate their wool.'"[27]

Critics thus condemned a wide range of writers for their portrayals of African Americans. Representations ranged from Stowe's paternalistic account of loyal and childlike slaves to virulent racist portraits of African Americans during Reconstruction to burlesques of African American social pretensions among contemporary authors. What all of these writers had in common was, according to critics, a refusal to "see more than skin-deep—the grin, the grimace and the picturesque externalities." The Negro was not a real person; he had neither depth nor character. For many of these writers, "Negro life was a shuttlecock between the two extremes of humor and pathos," according to Braithwaite.[28] They offered neither complex nor heterogeneous accounts of African Americans, preferring instead to paint their characters in broad strokes.

Picturing the Old Negro

The Plantation School writers and later authors all wrote during what Daniel Boorstin calls the Graphic Revolution, which began during the second half of the nineteenth century. Changes in technology—the development of cheap printing, the mechanization of many aspects of book publishing—fostered a rapid increase in book and magazine publication and in newspaper circulation.[29] These and other improvements in "technological reproducibility" enabled the easy reproduction of images in print—in advertising, magazines, newspapers, and literary texts.[30] As Boorstin writes, "Man's ability to make, preserve, transmit, and disseminate precise images—images of print, of men and landscapes and events, of the voices of men and mobs—now grew at a fantastic pace."[31] This Graphic Revolution set the stage for what scholars have termed the "Golden Age of Illustration," extending roughly from the 1870s through the early 1900s.[32]

Henry Louis Gates is thus onto something when he concludes his now classic article "The Trope of a New Negro and the Reconstruction of the Image of the Black" with a "visual essay."[33] Though he does not articulate the point directly, he recognizes the importance of visual coding in the economy of racial representation in the nineteenth century. Visual images, present in advertisements, postcards, magazine and novel illustrations, sheet music, posters, and lithographs, were paramount in codifying ideas of race.

Images of African Americans proliferated in magazine advertisements. Pictures of grinning black children were used to sell everything from gelatin to soap to baking soda.[34] Currier and Ives, America's premier lithography firm, produced a series of images entitled *Distinguished Colored Men of 1883,* which included portraits of the great African American men of the Reconstruction era.[35] It also issued a series of comic caricatures, entitled *Darktown,* from the mid-1870s to the early 1890s. These lithographs, which were marketed to the middle and working classes, were found in firehouses, barbershops, hotels, poolrooms, and other commercial and public spaces. They burlesqued all aspects of black life, from sports and games to marriage, political participation, and literary interest, and they exaggerated the bodies and behaviors of African Americans.[36] The series was extremely popular; the graphic artist who produced most of the images, Thomas Worth, claimed that 73,000 copies of one print in the series were sold.[37]

Despite this variety of visual images and their placement in an enormous range of venues, literary critics and art historians saw two illustrators—E. W. Kemble and A. B. Frost—as particularly problematic for their imagination of the Old Negro. Rather than identifying the Old Negro with the politicians featured in *Distinguished Colored Men* (as the *Messenger* might have in 1919) or with the exaggerated figures in the *Darktown* series or in advertisements (as twenty-first-century viewers might), Harlem Renaissance and later critics condemned the images produced by those two illustrators.

The names Kemble and Frost appeared in 1920s critical reflections on past representations of African Americans. Kemble is the only visual artist mentioned by Braithwaite, who links him to Octavus Roy Cohen and sees his work as a part of a long history of socially and aesthetically suspect representations: "A little later with the vogue of the 'darkey-story,' and its devotees from Kemble and McAllister to Octavus Roy Cohen, sentimental comedy in the portrayal of the Negro similarly degenerated to blatant but diverting farce. Before the rise of a new attitude, these represented the bottom reaction, both in artistic and social attitude. Reconstruction fiction was passing out in a flood of propagandist melodrama and ridicule."[38] Emmett Scott believed that Kemble, whom he likened to Thomas Nelson Page, had a nefarious influence on contemporary writers. He wrote that Macfall, "moulded years ago in the school of Kemble and Thomas Nelson Page, sees Negroes only as a strange class of creatures, aping the actions of white people."[39]

That Kemble and Frost were known as illustrators of African Americans certainly accounts for the interest of literary critics in their works (although writings by Stowe, Page, Dixon, and others were illustrated by many other graphic artists). Yet even later art historians identified them as particularly egregious purveyors of the Old Negro. In 1943, James Porter, who wrote the first survey of African American art, saw the pair as an integral part of nineteenth-century popular graphic-art portrayals of African Americans. In language strikingly similar to that of his 1920s predecessors, Porter stated:

> White writers of the time appeared determined to perpetuate the traditional southern conception of the Negro, and their influence was one of the viciously repressive factors on the improvement of race relations in early Twentieth Century southern society. The indifference or hostility of most white Americans to the cultural betterment of the Negro is mirrored in the literature of the late Reconstruction era and the first decade of the Twentieth Century. The portrayal of Negro character by southern fiction writers and illustrators, for example, dealt only with the fabulous, comical, quaint, or criminal side of Negro personality. This was especially true of the school of Thomas Dixon and Thomas Nelson Page, which set the pattern for the fictionalized Negro in that "plantation ideology" still evident in the writings of Octavus Roy Cohen. Such writers were ably seconded by illustrators of the stamp of A. B. Frost

and E. W. Kemble, who immortalized "Uncle Toms," "Aunt Chloes," "Rastuses," and other overdrawn "darky" or villainous types.[40]

Kemble was an extraordinarily prolific, albeit limited, illustrator. He first gained national notoriety by illustrating Mark Twain's *Adventures of Huckleberry Finn,* thereby firmly establishing his career as the "delineator" of the Negro.[41] He illustrated sixty-seven books, fifty-eight of which have images of African Americans.[42] These included Joel Chandler Harris' *Daddy Jake, The Runaway,* and *Short Stories Told after Dark,* and Paul Laurence Dunbar's *"Strength of Gideon" and Other Stories* and *The Heart of Happy Hollow.* He provided illustrations for Page's story "Two Little Confederates" in the magazine *St. Nicholas* (May 1888) and Cable's "Dance in Place Congo" in the *Century.*[43]

Kemble's representations of African Americans can be roughly grouped into two styles. For many of his illustrations, he created ethnic or racial "types," as he and others of the era called figurative studies. *Boy with Hands on Pole* is typical of one of Kemble's aesthetic styles (Figure 3). The hands are rendered sketchily and the feet not at all (it was well known that Kemble had difficulty drawing these basic elements of human physiognomy), and the child has slightly exaggerated features. *Old Mammy in Beauty Land* (Figure 4) is a study of an older African American woman—a racial type, as Kemble would say. It focuses on her face and could be a depiction of an actual, if unnamed, person. Kemble did a number of such sketches of non–African Americans, including *Georgia Cracker Types* (Figure 5), a study of Southern white men, and drawings of Irish people for Irwin Russell's *Christmas Night in the Quarters.* Kemble's images were remarkably consistent across the novels he illustrated, despite variations among the texts. His illustration of a young child (Figure 6) in Harris' *On the Plantation,* published in 1892, and of "Tom's baby" and other African American children in an 1892 edition of *Uncle Tom's Cabin* are nearly identical.

Kemble also worked in grotesque caricature, which hinges on exaggeration. In the years 1898 to 1901 he published *Coontown's 400, Comical Coons, Kemble's Pickaninnies,* and *Kemble's Blackberries.* These were comic picture books in which, as Joseph Boskin writes, African Americans appeared "round-faced and grinning, often in ragged clothing, beset by amusing yet trouble-some situations."[44]

Frost's illustrations were similar to Kemble's, although Harris thought Frost infinitely superior. He illustrated more than ninety books, including a number of Harris' Uncle Remus collections. For example, he produced 112 drawings for *Uncle Remus: His Songs and Sayings* (1895). In his illustrations for *Told by Uncle Remus: New Stories of the Old Plantation,* he depicted the animals that populated Uncle Remus' folktales, rather than the former slave himself or other characters in the stories.

Figure 3. E. W. Kemble, *Boy with Hands on Pole.* Between 1880 and 1933. Digital ID cai 2a13735, Prints and Photographs Division, Library of Congress.

Figure 4. E. W. Kemble, *Old Mammy in Beauty Land.* Between 1880 and 1933. Digital ID cai 2a13737, Prints and Photographs Division, Library of Congress.

Stereotyping the Old Negro

Although there were numerous nineteenth-century writers and artists who depicted African Americans, critics tended to focus on a select group. Why did Stowe, the Plantation School writers, Frost, and Kemble emerge as Old Negro purveyors when critics looked to the past? Braithwaite's reflections at the beginning of "The Negro in American Literature" offer us a clue:

> True to his origins on this continent, the Negro was projected into literature by an over-mastering and exploiting hand. In the generations that he has been so voluminously written and talked about he has been accorded as little artistic justice as social justice. Antebellum literature imposed the distortions of moralistic controversy and made the Negro a wax-figure of the market place: post-bellum literature retaliated with the condescending reactions of sentiment and caricature, and made the Negro a *genre* stereotype. Sustained, serious or deep study of Negro life and character has thus been entirely below the horizons of our national art. Only gradually, through the dull purgatory of the Age of Discussion, has Negro life eventually issued forth to an Age of Expression.[45]

Braithwaite's condemnation of these representations rests in part on his sense of their politics and political context. Certainly, the critic is right to point out how these novels, text and illustrations alike, participated in the racial discourse of their times. George Frederickson, in his account of racial thought in the United States from 1817 to 1914, *The Black Image in the White Mind,* describes how *Uncle Tom's Cabin* was part of a discourse of "romantic racialism," which was predicated on the idea of biological, rather than environmental or historical, differences among races and nationalities. Many elements in the work of Page, Dixon, Kemble, and others expressed ideas of paternalism or of racial difference that typified and buttressed the Jim Crow era, when segregation was emerging in the South.[46]

There were, however, great differences among these writers and illustrators, especially those grouped together under the "Plantation School" label. Frederickson points out that Cable, for example, decried racial stratification while calling for class stratification, while Dixon was particularly engaged with ideas of the "black brute."[47] Although Braithwaite, Brawley, and others articulated differences among the writers in their literary histo-

Figure 5. E. W. Kemble, *Georgia Cracker Types.* Illustration for "The Georgia Cracker in the Cotton Mills," *Century Illustrated Monthly Magazine,* February 1891. Reproduction no. LC-USZ62-84854, Prints and Photographs Division, Library of Congress.

Figure 6. E. W. Kemble, *The Door Attendant*. Illustration for Joel Chandler Harris, *On the Plantation*, 1892. Collection of the author.

ries, perhaps something other than their diverse political contexts and ideas about race caused critics to lump them together.

Braithwaite's antipathy to authors who create "wax-figure[s] of the market place" and Brawley's complaint that Harris and Cable "embalmed vanished or vanishing types" suggest that the critics objected to the mechanism by which these representations operated.[48] Specifically, the critics objected to the way in which literary and visual images, ranging from "caricature" to "sentiment," made the Negro into a "*genre* stereotype."

The word "stereotype" is the key here, because it is the valence of racial representation that most troubled Harlem Renaissance and later critics. Locke, in "American Literary Tradition and the Negro," writes: "The North, having been fed only on stereotypes, came to ignore the Negro in any intimate or critical way through the deceptive influence of those very stereotypes."[49] In *Negro Art: Past and Present,* published in 1936, he bemoans these nineteenth-century representations:

> The "old faithful uncle,"—later Uncle Tom, Uncle Ned, and Uncle Remus, the broad expansive "mammy" from Aunt Chloe to Aunt Jemima, the jiggling plantation hand in tattered jeans and the sprawling pickaninnies all became the typical stereotypes, and scarcely any Nineteenth Century art show was without its genre portrait study of one or more of these types or its realistically painted or sketched portrayal of *"The Plantation Quarters"* or *"Ole Virginia Life"* or some such glorification of the slave system.[50]

Poet and critic Sterling Brown also introduces this concept in his 1937 book *The Negro in American Fiction:* "We shall see in this study how stereotypes—that the Negro is *all* this, that, or the other—have evolved at the dictates of social policy."[51] Yet it is puzzling that caricature (like the Currier and Ives *Darktown* series or Aunt Jemimah or "sprawling pickaninnies") and sentiment (as in the mawkish depictions in *Uncle Tom's Cabin*) receive less attention than stereotype.

Stereotype, caricature, and other forms of figurative representation (in both literary and visual form) rely on recognizability; like the portrait, they portray their subjects so that their audiences can identify images with the subjects to which they allude.[52] Yet whereas caricature operates by exaggerating gestures, physiognomy, and behavior of the human figure, sometimes to impossible extremes, stereotype hinges on a pretense of verisimilitude and repetition. It becomes problematic, for although it maintains some claim on "reality" through aesthetic strategies that allow figures to seem familiar—physiognomically, behaviorally, or emotionally—and hence possible, it erases individuality.

Werner Sollor's essay "Was Roxy Black?," Sander Gilman's *Difference and Pathology,* and E. H. Gombrich's *Art and Illusion* are particularly helpful here. Caricature, which comes, Sollors writes, "from Italian *caricare,* 'to load, charge, exaggerate,'" must bear a likeness of what it represents, though it may be a "grotesquely exaggerated likeness."[53] Gilman tells us that stereotype is "a crude set of mental representations of the world . . . [that] perpetuate a needed sense of difference between the 'self' and the 'object,' which becomes the Other."[54] Gombrich writes that this "mental set" forms a vocabulary with which writers and artists may "embark on a 'copy' of reality."[55] But stereotypes emerge in "texts," broadly construed, when writers or artists fail to move beyond this received vocabulary.[56] Despite the differences in the way they operate, caricature (which can become stereotype) and stereotype both require an apparent association with an external subject. Sollors remarks, "To be recognizable, such images have to comment on a reality that they distort but *still represent recognizably.*"[57]

Stereotype's insistence on the recognizability of its subjects as humans, albeit deformed by cliché, rather than on the recognizability of its subject as human, mediated through "clouds of lines" (as Gombrich writes of visual caricature),[58] points to what I call its realist logic. Stereotype works by containing the pretense of accuracy and hence authority—something that Harlem Renaissance critics saw as particularly problematic, for they recognized that this realist logic, this claim on mimesis, is in fact flawed. Locke identified this problem in the work of Page and Cable. He wrote, "Beginning with good genre drawing that had the promise of something, they ended in mediocre chromographic romanticism."[59] A chromograph is essentially a nineteenth-century copy machine.[60] While Page and Cable may have had the potential to depict scenes from ordinary life, their worked merely repeated "romanticism." Sollors' understanding of stereotype explains Locke's discomfort: "In its force as a preexisting, stable mental image that is projected upon a more complicated and changing reality, the artistic 'stereotype'—the term derives from a printing process in which a cast mold is used instead of the forme itself, hence designating 'something continued or constantly repeated without change' *(Oxford English Dictionary)*—runs against more 'realistic' and 'individualized' perceptions of the world."[61] Thus, while a stereotype may seem to depict "accurately" racial, ethnic, religious, national, or other groups, it in fact denies complexity and heterogeneity through its formulaic and uniform expressions.

Stowe claimed that her Uncle Tom was an accurate, realistic representation, despite the fact that he could be seen as an exaggerated vision of black docility. Consider, for example, her remarks at the conclusion of the text:

> The writer has often been inquired of, by correspondents from different parts of the country, whether this narrative is a true one; and to these inquiries she will give one general answer.

> The separate incidents that compose the narrative are to a very great extent authentic, occurring, many of them, either under her own observation or that of her personal friends. She or her friends have observed characters the counterpart of almost all that are here introduced; and many of the sayings are word for word as heard herself, or reported to her.
>
> The personal appearance of Eliza, the character ascribed to her, are sketched drawn from life. The incorruptible fidelity, piety, and honesty of Uncle Tom had more than one development, to her personal knowledge.[62]

This assertion—that she is writing about slaves she has known—is part of a mimetic claim for her work. Moreover, Stowe casts Uncle Tom as typical of his race: "Tom, who had the soft, impressible nature of his kindly race, ever yearning toward the simple and childlike, watched the little creatures with daily increasing interest."[63] And again: "Tom got down from the carriage, and looked about with an air of calm, still enjoyment. The negro, it must be remembered, is an exotic of the most gorgeous and superb countries of the world, and he has, deep in his heart, a passion for all that is splendid, rich and fanciful; a passion which, rudely indulged by an untrained taste, draws on them the ridicule of the colder and more correct white race."[64] Uncle Tom, in both of these descriptions, embodies "his kindly race" and "the negro." Rather than appearing in the text as an individual, he stands for a category "through which we [in this case, the non–African American author] label and classify the Other," to use Gilman's words.

Stowe was not alone in claiming that her characters were truthful portrayals. Harris wrote in the introduction to his first collection of Uncle Remus tales: "Each legend has its variants, but in every instance I have retained that particular version which seemed to me to be the most characteristic, and have given it without embellishment and without exaggeration. The dialect, it will be observed, is wholly different from that of the Hon. Pompey Smash and his literary descendants, and different also from the intolerable misrepresentations of the minstrel stage, but it is at least phonetically genuine."[65] Moreover, he asserts that one of his stories, "A Story of the War," is "almost literally true."[66] Dixon wrote of *The Leopard's Spots*: "It may shock the prejudices of those who have idealized or worshiped the negro as canonized in 'Uncle Tom.' Is it not time they heard the whole truth? They have heard only one side for forty years."[67] Interestingly, both Harris and Dixon position their work against earlier texts, which contain "misrepresentations."

Kemble also claimed authority for his visual images. Reflecting back on his long career, he wrote in the 1930s:

I was established as a delineator of the South, the Negro being my specialty, and, as I have mentioned, I had never been South at all. I didn't go for two years more. Then I told Mr. Gilder that it was high time for me to go and see what the real article looked like. He agreed with me. After visiting several plantations and noting the local color, a thing I had missed but had not attempted to carry out to any extent in my pictures, I found that my types were, in most cases, the counterparts of those surrounding me.[68]

Kemble's language points to what he imagined his illustrations would accomplish. Despite never having visited the South, his "types" were in fact kin to the "real article," and thus "real" representations in and of themselves.

Harris did not approve of Kemble's work, precisely because of the artist's interest in types. Harris wrote in the *Atlanta Constitution,* on September 26, 1892: "For a man who has no conception whatever of human nature, Kemble does very well. But he is too doggoned flip to suit me. . . . Neither fiction nor illustrative art has any business with types. It must address itself to life, to the essence of life, which is character, which is individuality."[69] Harris recognized the limits of types (as Kemble termed them) or stereotypes (as later critics denoted them). Although he did not imagine that they operated in his own work, he saw how Kemble's images erased individuality despite assertions to the contrary.

The assumption that his representations were true-to-life bled into Kemble's caricatures, which are exaggerated to such a degree that one might well think they lack authority. Yet one critic wrote, in an essay entitled "Family Pride, or Art for Life's Sake," published in *Life* in December 1896: "When it comes to Kemble's coons, the spirit of mirth is let loose. From the big-eyed pickaninny to the toothless old mammy, the Southern Negro goes laughing through the pages. The Northern man who gets his ideas of Negroes from the minstrel stage will have a shaking up when he sees Kemble's real plantation darkies—as various and 'consequencious' as white folks."[70]

When text and image meet in an illustrated book, stereotype's authoritative claims grow even stronger. Sollors reminds us that illustration is "derived from Latin *illustrare,* 'to light up, illuminate, clear up,'" and means the "pictorial elucidation of any subject; the elucidation or embellishment of a literary or scientific article, book, etc. by pictorial representation." J. Hillis Miller also calls attention to this definition: "The word means bringing to light, as a spelunker lights up a cave, or as a medieval manuscript is illuminated."[71] For illustrations to "work," Sollors argues, they must "remain in an intelligible relation to characters from the text."[72]

Following the expiration of its copyright in 1891, Stowe's *Uncle Tom's Cabin* went through numerous illustrated versions. Kemble illustrated the 1892 edition, providing 121 line drawings of characters and scenes from the book and sixteen photogravures, mostly of the characters and some of landscapes. The text and illustrations—"two kinds of signs," as Miller calls them—buttress each other, by working both separately and in conjunction to claim authenticity and authority for the depictions of African Americans.[73] The images confirm the text, and the text, in turn, confirms the illustrations. In many respects, this structure follows that of slave narratives, which were authenticated by ancillary material, such as portraits, letters, and other documents that attested to the identity of the authors.[74]

Stowe recognized the claims that visual imagery seemed to have on authenticity, and shows this in the way she first introduces Uncle Tom to her readers. She claims to "daguerreotype" him, employing a term that connoted an objective representation, "a mirror" (as Oliver Wendell Holmes wrote in 1859) of the world:[75]

> At this table was seated Uncle Tom, Mr. Shelby's best hand, who, as he is to be the hero of our story, we must daguerreotype for our readers. He was a large, broad-chested, powerfully made man, of a full glossy black, and a face whose truly African features were characterized by an expression of grave and steady good sense, united with much kindliness and benevolence. There was something about his whole air self-respecting and dignified, yet united with a confiding and humble simplicity.[76]

This literary daguerreotype is a description of physical form that bleeds into an assessment of Tom's character and his racial identity.

The images that Kemble provided of Tom and other characters resemble their descriptions. They are recognizable but so remarkably similar that they fix or set racial representation. Consider his photogravures of Aunt Chloe and Uncle Tom. Because photogravures are essentially crosses between photographs and lithographs, they contain a presumption of accuracy, despite the obvious manipulation by the artist.[77] In the photogravure *Tom and His Children* (Figure 7), placed opposite the description of Tom's "gentle, domestic heart, which . . . has been a peculiar characteristic of his unhappy race," Tom is at the center of the composition. His face is downcast, his eyes closed, and his hands clasped as he stands near his sleeping children, evoking the "confiding and humble simplicity" of Stowe's description. Light emanates from the left side of the frame so that Tom's forehead is paler than the rest of his face, as is the forehead of one of the sleeping children. These patches of light are the visual equivalent of the "full

Figure 7. E. W. Kemble, *Tom and His Children*. Illustration for Harriet Beecher Stowe, *Uncle Tom's Cabin, or Life among the Lowly*, 1892. Collection of the author.

Figure 8. E. W. Kemble, *Under the Orange Trees*. Illustration for Harriet Beecher Stowe, *Uncle Tom's Cabin, or Life among the Lowly*, 1892. Collection of the author.

Figure 9. E. W. Kemble, *Aunt Chloe*. Illustration for Harriet Beecher Stowe, *Uncle Tom's Cabin, or Life among the Lowly*, 1892. Collection of the author.

glossy black." Tom's "African features," undefined in the text, are also undefined in the image.

Kemble's illustrations not only reflected description of physical appearance but also scenes from the plot. A line drawing of Tom carrying Eva supports the account of Uncle Tom carrying the girl shortly before her death (Figure 8). His stance is similar to that in the photogravure. Thus, the visual image relates both to Stowe's description and to the other illustration. Text and description work together to portray Tom.

Yet when we examine the description and photogravure of Aunt Chloe (Figure 9), we can see the emergence of a pattern within the text and the images. Stowe writes: "A round, black, shining face is hers, so glossy as to suggest the idea that she might have been washed over with white of eggs, like one of her own teas rusks. Her whole plump countenance beams with satisfaction and contentment, under her well-starched checkered turban, bearing on it, however, if we must confess it, a little of that tinge of self-consciousness which becomes the first cook of the neighborhood, as Aunt Chloe was universally held and acknowledged to be."[78] The language is similar to that of the description of Tom. Both have "glossy," "black" faces. The photogravure of Aunt Chloe, which catches her as she bakes, likewise suggests glossiness through the manipulation of light and through the contrast between her black skin and the milk she pours. Although the image of Aunt Chloe refers to Stowe's description of her physical appearance and of her position as "first cook of the neighborhood," it also bears some affinity to the image of Aunt Jemimah, which emerges in 1890.[79]

Gilman tells us that the structure of stereotype emerges in a social or political context when the "Other" is "externalized"; every "social group has a set vocabulary of images for this externalized Other."[80] The static literary and visual vocabularies of Stowe and Kemble point to the construction of a stereotype. In 1922, Walter Lippmann, a contemporary of the Harlem Renaissance critics, pointed to the danger of stereotype. He devoted a quarter of his book *Public Opinion* to the concept of the stereotype, articulating the conceptual danger that Harlem Renaissance and later critics saw in the diverse literary and visual representations of the Old Negro. He described the way in which stereotype structures an understanding of the world by providing fixed and hence simplified representations. "For the most part we do not first see, and then define, we define first and then see. In the great blooming, buzzing confusion of the outer world we pick out what our culture has already defined for us, and we tend to perceive that which we have picked out in the form stereotyped for us by our culture."[81] The problem is the air of believability attributed to the stereotype—"our gullibility," he calls it—and its remarkable persistence. "A stereotype may be so consistently and authoritatively transmitted in each generation from parent to child that it seems almost like a biological fact."[82]

Charles S. Johnson followed Lippmann's lead in an article entitled "Public Opinion and the Negro." He describes the dangers of "time-saving generalizations, stereotypes, myths, conventions, dogma" about African American identity.[83] "Jokes about Negroes, news stories, anecdotes, gossip, the stage, the motion pictures, the Octavus Roy Cohen, Hugh Wiley and Irvin S. Cobb type of humorous fiction repeated with unvarying outline, have helped to build up and crystallize a fictitious being unlike any Negro. Usually one of two things happens when a Negro fails to reflect this type: Either he is considered an exception or he is 'out of his place.'"[84] Rather than imagining a new Negro, based on experience, individuals maintain their preconceived stereotypes—the "picture within our heads" —which enable them to maintain ideas of "recognition, of classification, and of behavior itself."[85]

Literary and visual stereotypes, which prey on clichés of group identity, and their conjunction in illustrated texts deeply troubled critics precisely because they failed to offer a sense of the heterogeneity of the African American population and because they could be construed as "fact." Locke claimed, "If it ever was warrantable to regard and treat the Negro en masse, it is becoming with every day less possible, more unjust and more ridiculous." It was time for Negroes to be "seriously portrayed and painted," by themselves and by whites.[86] In the decades to come, writers, artists, and critics would tackle literary and visual stereotypes by recasting ideas of African American identity, folk culture, and history.

chapter two

Enter the New Negro

ARLY IN 1924, Charles S. Johnson—black intellectual, editor of *Opportunity*, author of *Shadow of the Plantation*, and major figure in the Harlem Renaissance—felt compelled to mark publicly something he had discerned in his circle of acquaintances.[1] Johnson was a member of a "little group which meets . . . to talk informally about 'books and things.'" He had recently observed a change, a "growing self-consciousness," in the group's conversations and decided to hold a dinner to celebrate "this newer school of writers," which included Eric Walrond, Countee Cullen, Langston Hughes, and Gwendolyn Bennett.[2]

Johnson wrote to Alain Locke asking him to be the master of ceremonies, an invitation which ultimately led to Locke's crowning as the culture-broker for the era.[3] Locke agreed to attend. In March 1924, the current and future leaders of African America, a number of New York City's white literati, and others gathered at New York City's Civic Club. Attendees included members of the little group as well as other notables, including Eugene O'Neill, Carl Van Doren, W. E. B. Du Bois, and H. L. Mencken.[4] Officially, the dinner fêted Jessie Fauset, literary editor of the *Crisis*, who had recently published a novel entitled *There Was Confusion.*[5] Johnson, however, turned the focus of the occasion toward the younger generation of African American writers and artists.

Many prominent individuals spoke, including W. E. B. Du Bois and publisher Horace Liveright, who, with the Boni brothers, had published Jean Toomer's *Cane* in 1923. Carl Van Doren, editor of *Century* magazine and a professor at Columbia, delivered a speech entitled "The Younger Generation of Negro Writers" in which he heralded "the new literary age, for which the Negroes of the country are in a remarkable strategic position."[6] Yet of all the individuals present, Locke took center stage. Acting as the master of ceremonies, he celebrated his membership in the younger generation of black writers.

Among the guests was the greatly impressed Paul Kellogg, the editor of the *Survey*, a weekly magazine devoted to "social interpretation" and aimed at social workers. Since the magazine was devoted to following "the subtle traces of race growth and interaction through the shifting outline of social organization and by the flickering light of individual achievement," it is unsurprising that he found an idea for a special issue of the *Survey Graphic*, the monthly edition of the *Survey*, at the gathering of young African American literati.[7] In a letter to Dr. D. W. Alexander, Kellogg wrote that he had been at a "meeting in honor of a young Negro writer at which musicians, poets, composers, scientists, social workers, men and women of the professions were present. It struck me that this afforded a new approach which we might employ in a special number in such a way as to, shall I say revisualize the phenomena of these new northern communities of black folk."[8]

Following the event, Kellogg proposed that Locke serve as guest editor for a special issue of the magazine, to be devoted to the burgeoning New Negro movement in Harlem. Locke accepted the offer, and in March 1925 the *Survey Graphic* published its New Negro issue. Entitled "Harlem: Mecca of the New Negro," it was "a full-length study of the New Negro" and sold more than 40,000 copies in two printings.[9] At the end of 1925, Albert and Charles Boni, Inc., published an expanded version of the magazine in book form. Locke edited the lengthy volume, entitled *The New Negro: An Interpretation*. This was an anthology of essays, creative writing, and images; some were from the *Survey Graphic* and others had been commissioned for the anthology or reprinted from other magazines. Writing in 1926, in anticipation of the second printing of the collection (1927), critic Leon Whipple wrote that *The New Negro* was "comprehensive, full of passion and faith, brimming with fact and new viewpoints, and starkly clear in its revelation that there is a 'new Negro,' keenly and naturally at times bitterly aware of himself and his place in our civilization."[10]

From the Survey Graphic

The *Survey Graphic* issue and the two subsequent printings of *The New Negro* heralded the Harlem Renaissance and celebrated its hero, the New Negro.[11] The three versions are similar, containing a number of the same articles and illustrations, and the two printings of the anthology are nearly identical. Yet the differences between the magazine and the anthology and between the two printings of the anthology are telling, for they reveal how Locke, an extraordinarily significant critic, strove to expand the conventions of racial representation during the Harlem Renaissance.

It may be tempting to attribute the shifts between the magazine and the anthologies to the circumstances of their publication.[12] After all, editors tinker with their work often and for a variety of reasons. Moreover, the process of transforming a single issue of a magazine into a book-length anthology is complicated and somewhat predetermined. Editors may include new material or change the format of old material to accommodate the physical characteristics of the book or the demands of publishers. In addition, books, especially popular ones, often go through second printings; editors, publishers, and authors may correct mistakes or add new material.

Locke made many mechanical changes of this sort when he revised the magazine for the 1925 anthology, which he modified for the 1927 printing. Yet he also made a number of changes in substance and tone. Locke moved from the documentary agenda of the *Survey Graphic* to a *belles-lettres* sensibility in *The New Negro,* including fiction, poetry, and art that showcased the "younger generation" of African American writers and artists. The differences between the two printings of the anthology are subtle. Locke added two poems, changed the location of some photographs of African masks, and added books to the bibliography. One change, however, was dramatic: he placed a significant number of new drawings by the young African American artist Aaron Douglas in the second printing of *The New Negro,* suggesting that more than simple mechanical revisions were at stake.

These shifts were components of Locke's editorial experiments in constructing a literary and visual vocabulary adequate for the New Negro. They suggest that Locke was attempting to formulate—through word and image—new ways of imagining African American identity. He was seeking new voices and new faces for the race, in contrast to the limiting representations of the past, when the Negro was seen through "the dusty spectacles of past controversy" and "typical stereotypes"—uncles, aunties, pickaninnies, and others—were in vogue.[13] In this light, the *Survey Graphic* and the two printings of *The New Negro* form a series, acting as a single aesthetic object in material flux over time and an invaluable lens with which to examine debates about race, realism, modernism, and the New Negro.

Locke's New Negro Program

As the editor and most prominent (some may say ubiquitous) essayist of the magazine, Locke directs a specific reading of the New Negro phenomenon.[14] His opening articles and his introductions to the work of others elucidate his ideas about race, aesthetics, and the sea change he perceived in the African American population. Locke's essays "Harlem" and "Enter the New Negro" open the main body of the *Survey Graphic*. These pieces, which he combined into one longer essay for *The New Negro,* offer a "dramatic . . . glimpse of the New Negro" and discuss myriad concerns relevant to the African American population of the 1920s, including stereotypes of the past, segregation, industrialization, and even Marcus Garvey's contemporary nationalistic movement. Yet several consistent themes emerge. Locke situates the New Negro, or rather New Negroes, within a broad context: the development of Harlem as a national and international racial center, the shifts in the psychology of African Americans toward a racial consciousness, and the concomitant moves in arts and letters—a central element in the participation of African Americans in American democratic life.

In "Harlem," Locke paints a picture of 1920s Harlem and its residents—a "race capital" inhabited by "the greatest Negro community the world has known." Populated by the Great Migration of African Americans from the rural South and the influx of "so many diverse elements of Negro life, . . . the African, the West Indian, the Negro American," Harlem is home to a huge variety of people—"the Negro of the North and the Negro of the South; the man from the city and the man from the town and village; the peasant, the student, the business man, the professional man, artist, poet, musician, adventurer and worker, preacher and criminal, exploiter and social outcast." Out of this multitude, these diverse people streaming to Harlem for "social and economic freedom," a "group expression and self-determination" is beginning to emerge. Harlem, "significant" and "prophetic," is the site of "racial awakening," a place where "Negro life is not only founding new centers, but finding a new soul." This mass of people and their new sense of themselves as a people would be the subject of the *Survey Graphic*'s New Negro issue. The contributors, both writers and artists, would "voice these new aspirations of a people, . . . read the clear message of the new conditions, and . . . discuss some of the new relationships and contracts they involve."[15]

Locke's essay "Enter the New Negro" is a plea for the recognition of the centrality of African Americans in the United States and indeed the world.

The Negro community—in the process of developing a "new mentality," a "new psychology," and a "new spirit," in contrast the Old Negro, who was "more of a myth than a man"—is a central part of American democracy, Locke claims. African Americans reach for "nothing but American wants, American ideas" via "race values." This "unique social experiment" is an effort to open up democracy and to see "American ideals progressively fulfilled." Yet Harlem is also an international center, "home of the Negro's 'Zionism.'" African Americans are thus both a central element in the development of a multiracial American democracy and "the advance-guard of the African peoples in their contact with Twentieth Century civilization."[16]

Locke makes three central moves in these two essays. First, he stresses the heterogeneity of the African American population, which, despite differences within, is engaged in the development of a racial sensibility. He lists Harlem denizens: "the Negro poet, student, artist, thinker," "the clergyman following his errant flock, the physician or lawyer trailing his clients," "the reformers, the fighting advocates, the inner spokesmen, the poets, artists, and social prophets," along with the "migrant masses."[17] Second, Locke decries the failure of "The Sociologist, The Philanthropist, the Race-Leader" to account for this heterogeneity and for the growing group consciousness. No longer would society accept limiting "formulae": the Negro as "something to be argued about, condemned or defended, to be 'kept down,' or 'in his place,' or 'helped up,' to be worried with or worried over, harassed or patronized, a social bogey or a social burden"—"unjust stereotypes" all. He calls for an expansion of received notions of African American identity—"obsolete" opinions. Certain phrases—such as "the Negro today wishes to be known for what he is, even his faults and shortcomings," and "with the Negro rapidly in process of class differentiation, if it ever was warrantable to regard and treat the Negro en masse, it is becoming with every day less possible, more unjust and more ridiculous"—suggest that he and his fellow writers and artists in the magazine will offer a fuller account of African American life, a "realistic facing of the facts." Third, Locke claims that arts and letters are crucial to "rehabilitating the race in world esteem from that loss of prestige for which the fate and conditions of slavery have so largely been responsible." What will persuade both blacks and whites of the centrality of Negro life on the American and world stages is the "revaluation . . . of the Negro in terms of his artistic endowments and cultural contributions, past and present." These ideas would all surface in the magazine, since it would include a variety of images and writings, which work together and individually to "survey" the New Negro phenomenon.[18]

Though we may be inclined to attribute to Locke all of the decisions about the production of the New Negro issue (given the strength of his editorial voice), by doing so, we fail to take into account the fact that questions of commercial viability, audience, and editorial process determined much of the appearance of the magazine and the anthologies. As the guest editor, Locke did direct the production of the *Survey Graphic* to a great degree. Yet sometimes his sense of what was important, necessary, or even aesthetically pleasing was subverted by the exigencies of production, for Locke had to follow established *Survey* patterns.

The *Survey* had grown out of the Pittsburgh magazine *Charities and the Commons*. In the early 1900s, *Charities* had produced a number of special issues. In 1904, it had brought out one on immigration; in 1905, it had published another entitled "The Negro in Cities of the North," which had included writings by Booker T. Washington and Du Bois.

In 1909, the editors, including brothers Arthur and Paul Kellogg, had renamed the magazine the *Survey*.[19] In 1915, Paul Kellogg had written that the primary aim of the magazine was to be "an investigator and interpreter of the objective conditions of life and labor and . . . a chronicler of undertakings to improve them." Because the magazine aimed for such complete and objective accounting of its subject, it used a large quantity of pictorial material, including "photographs and sketches, maps, charts, graphs, tables, and diagrams."[20]

In 1923, the Kelloggs had created the *Survey Graphic,* a monthly magazine which aspired to be "a frank experiment in the technique of social interpretation."[21] It addressed the general public, rather than professional social workers, but continued the *Survey*'s tradition of using visual sources. According to historian Clarke Chambers, its aim was "to engage the attention of a wide audience by use of graphic and literary arts in partnership with the social sciences, to catch the eye and the heart, as well as the intellect."[22] Indeed, the interartistic logic of the *Survey Graphic* rests on the conception of the "survey" itself, the formula on which the magazine relied. Meant to be a panorama of "social facts gathered by trained investigators and presented to the public in word and image," the survey aimed to document and to record, with ostensible accuracy and a degree of authority, social movements and diverse peoples.[23]

The *Survey Graphic* published material on groups undergoing social, demographic change. The editors put out issues on Mexican and Irish nationalism, gypsies, and other groups striving for self-determination. Such people constituted the "human variety" that was the magazine's specialty.[24] These were ethnic, racial, or national "types"—meaning groups distinct from the readers of the magazine.[25] The heterogeneous New Negroes experiencing a surge in group consciousness, as described by Locke, accorded perfectly with the magazine's conception.

In contrast to the stereotypes rejected by Harlem Renaissance critics, "types," in *Survey Graphic* parlance, did not necessarily mean figures who were unique or actual individuals; rather, they epitomized group characteristics and could reveal the effects of history or socioeconomic position.[26] The magazine presented these types with reportorial or sociological essays and with naturalistic drawings meant to depict "typical" figures (rather than real-life individuals). Such drawings were labeled "type sketches."

A good part of the New Negro issue focuses on the social situation of African Americans, using standard *Survey Graphic* techniques. James Weldon Johnson's "Making of Harlem" and Charles S. Johnson's "Black Workers and the City" are classic examples of the magazine's essayistic style. The articles are sociological in approach and historically focused, and make claims about the socioeconomic positions of blacks. Photographs, maps, and figurative drawings are mixed with the text. Each of these images claims a realistic perspective akin to that of the articles.[27]

James Weldon Johnson's article describes Harlem as a "great Mecca" for the entire Negro world. It is "not a colony or community," a slum quarter, or any other subset of New York, but a "city within a city." This description places Negroes at the center of Harlem life and asserts that Harlem, because it has its own institutions, is equivalent to other American cities. In fact, Johnson declares that there is "no change, indeed, in the appearance of the people, except in their color."[28] Yet Harlem is unique because it is product of both discriminatory practice and Negro self-assertion.

Johnson supports his claim in a variety of ways. He describes the history of Harlem's growth, detailing the patterns of migration from lower Manhattan. He discusses the employment prospects of the Negro in New York and describes the city's "economic and industrial situation." Maintaining a sociological tone, he even reports the price of houses and the exact physical boundaries of Harlem. He asserts that Harlem is "a Negro community," "typically Negro" but with "unique characteristics," where African Americans are experiencing "a constant growth of group consciousness and community feeling." A "type," for Johnson, is a figure that exhibits the effects of the socioeconomic situation of Harlem.[29]

Photographs of rush hour at the intersection of 135th Street and Lenox Avenue and of Striver's Row punctuate the text of the article. These are not art photographs; rather, they offer information, as suggested by the long captions underneath them (a map of Harlem does the same thing). The photograph *Harlem Doorway* (Figure 10) presents a woman standing at the entrance to a Harlem building, looking away from the camera. Another image, *Looking toward the Lafayette Theatre on Seventh Avenue,* is a study of a man walking down the street. Both photos are informative of the "types" Johnson describes. They do not stand alone but act as illustrative, contextual material, situated within the columns of the article itself.[30]

Charles S. Johnson's "Black Workers and the City" employs a tone and focus similar to that of James Weldon Johnson's article but complicates the notion of types. Charles S. Johnson discusses the history of black labor in New York City and the variety of Harlem's workers. He writes about the concrete and historical issues facing blacks in New York City—the economic aspects of Negro-Irish interactions, the New York draft riots, barriers to union membership—and calls for sounder economic policy.[31]

What is most interesting about Charles Johnson's article is the way in which he undermines notions of national racial homogeneity with a rhetoric of "types" different from that of James Weldon Johnson. He writes that the population of Harlem is "one part native, one part West Indian and about three parts Southern." This, he asserts, has "changed the whole complexion and outlook of the Negro New Yorker." But New York Negroes are more different from Southern Negroes than whites are from blacks, he claims.[32] This is because "the city creates his own types." Despite the fact that the Negro is a particular "type" vis-à-vis other ethnic groups, the Negro New Yorker is a "type" unto himself, rather than a stereotype of uniform Negro identity.[33] Because "cities have personalities," and because "chief industries are likely to determine not only respective characters, but the type of persons they attract and hold," the Negro workers in New York "defy racial classification." They do not and cannot stand in for all African Americans. Maintaining a social scientific tone, Johnson declares that "the Negro worker can no more become a fixed racial concept than can the white worker." The article details a broad and heterogeneous population of Negro workers, and focuses on their "predicament," which results from their industrial contact and economic competition with whites.[34]

Johnson's article claims that it is impossible to identify a single African American identity, a single "type," preferring the idea that there are many "types." Yet the illustration that accompanies the article—*The Laborer,* by

Figure 10. Anonymous, *Harlem Doorway*. Illustration for James Weldon Johnson, "The Making of Harlem," *Survey Graphic*, March 1925. Republished 1979; reproduced by permission of Black Classic Press.

Mahonri Young (Figure 11)—undermines this argument.[35] The drawing portrays a worker holding a tool of some sort, with his back to the viewer. His body is sculpted by muscles and appears very powerful. Because his face is directed away from the viewer, it is impossible to perceive any distinguishable features. Although Johnson denied a unitary and homogeneous African American working population, this single faceless black

Figure 11. Mahonri Young, *The Laborer*. Illustration for Charles S. Johnson, "Black Workers and the City," *Survey Graphic*, March 1925. Republished 1979; reproduced by permission of Black Classic Press.

worker seems to stand for all of the "black workers" of his title. The figure is a monolithic type—a model of all black workers, rather than one of the many individuals of that population. The figure and its caption stand for a mass, visually undermining Johnson's argument that a uniform mass does not exist.[36]

Although the *Survey Graphic* editors preferred to use photographic or naturalistic images and journalistic accounts to depict types, the New Negro issue employed a variety of media to present New Negro types: sociological essays, photographs, portraits focusing on composition and line, and even highly personal poems. This departure was Locke's contribution, and his first attempt to "seriously portray" the avatar of the Harlem Renaissance in the material published in the magazine and later in the two printings of the anthology.

The *Survey Graphic* included not only illustrated articles, but also independent visual examples of the New Negroes—images that claimed authority because of their realistic style. This independent presence of the graphic was as important to Locke as the presence of the verbal. So vital was it that the *Survey* sponsored a "*Survey Graphic* Harlem Art Contest," to get "representative interpretations of out contemporary race development and to use Harlem life as both its setting and its symbol." In a memo dated October 25, 1924, Locke provided publicity copy for the contest: "We feel that the contributions of the artists, as giving the graphic touch, will give great impetus to the public interest in the message."[37]

Locke's belief in the importance of using the visual to combat stereotypical or inaccurate representations was stated more explicitly in his essay "To Certain of Our Philistines," published in *Opportunity,* May 1925. "Of all the arts, painting is most bound by social ideas. And so, in spite of the fact that the Negro offers, in the line of the human subject, the most untouched of all the available fields of portraiture, and the most intriguing, if not indeed the most difficult of technical problems because of the variety of pigmentation and subtlety of values, serious painting has all but ignored him."[38] Locke's conviction that serious American portraiture had not yet taken up the formal demands of the African American subject is essential to understanding his commitment to the visual arts in the magazine and in the two printings of the anthology. Producing visual representations of African American identity was necessary because the fine arts were subject to great control by social mores: "Social conventions stand closer guard over painting than most of the other arts. It is for that reason that a new school and idiom of Negro portraiture is particularly significant."[39] Locke believed that something "new" in the realm of visual representation was necessary.

Editor Paul Kellogg seemed to believe that the best way to present the New Negro was to employ the type sketches for which the *Survey Graphic* was known. Kellogg asked Winold Reiss to contribute drawings, as he had done for earlier numbers.[40] Although Reiss had two sorts of work in the *Survey Graphic,* naturalistic portraits and impressionistic images about Harlem, he primarily contributed portraits, most of which are labeled "types."[41]

Reiss, a German émigré, had come to the United States in 1913.[42] Born in 1886, he had been educated at the Munich Academy of Fine Arts by Franz von Stuck, from whom Reiss seemed to adopt a number of elements of his portraiture.[43] His style and his interest in ethnographic "types" were also influenced by German art movements and by developments in German museum culture and the European art world. The mid-nineteenth century had seen the founding of ethnographic museums in a number of German cities, including Berlin, Leipzig, Dresden, and Munich. Thus, in Germany the interest was not only in the aesthetic aspects of so-called primitive art but also in the "exotic" peoples who produced this art.[44] Moreover, in the early years of the twentieth century, Cubist painters and others were becoming increasingly excited about Asian and African art. For example, the yearly *Blaue Reiter* almanacs (published by the Blaue Reiter school, a group of artists that included Wassily Kandinsky and Franz Marc) reproduced photos of African, Asian, Egyptian, Russian, Bavarian, and other folk art. Reiss was also influenced by a new style of German art called the Neue Sachlichkeit (New Objectivity). The aim of this movement was "exact and straightforward, three-dimensional depiction of the subject matter" that emphasized the "outer reality of the subject rather than the inner vision of the artist" and often depicted individuals in their work environments.[45] These contexts inspired Reiss's interest in the potential of painting to act simultaneously as ethnographic inquiry and aesthetic experimentation.[46]

Locke wrote the text accompanying Reiss's "Harlem Types"—seven "type sketches" that depicted residents of Harlem and that were published in the New Negro issue. Locke declared that Reiss was presenting a "graphic interpretation of Negro life, freshly conceived after its own patterns," and that he had "achieved what amounts to a revealing discovery of the significance, human and artistic, of one of the great dialects of human physiognomy, of some of the little-understood but powerful idioms of nature's speech."[47] Locke's metaphor—"dialects of human physiog-nomy"—suggests that he wanted to claim a visual vocabulary of race.

Reiss, Locke wrote, was "a folk-lorist of the brush and palette" who sought the "folk character back of the individual, the psychology behind the physiognomy." In his abstract design, Reiss found the "decorative ele-ments" and the "pattern of the culture from which [art] sprang." Reiss's talent was that "without the loss of naturalistic accuracy and individuality, he somehow subtly expresses the type, and without being any the less hu-man, captures the racial and the local."[48] In other words, Reiss's visual id-iom enabled him to juggle both the typical and the individual.

The conventions of art created two problems for artists interested in se-rious depictions of Negroes, Locke stated. What prevented the conven-tional artist from portraying the Negro were "certain narrowly arbitrary conventions of physical beauty, and, as well, that inevitable inscrutability of things seen but not understood." The other problem was caricature, which encouraged the "comic and grotesque" rather than "the serious, the tragic, the wistful."[49] Reiss's work thus won approval from Locke because he felt that it transcended convention.

The question is, of course, whether Reiss's drawings actually accomplish all that Locke asserts they do. His first drawing in the New Negro issue was *Congo: A Familiar of New York Studios* (Figure 12). It portrays a dis-embodied head staring out at the viewer. The face is framed by a full Afro that gives the impression of a halo. The effect is disconcerting, for the head looks almost like a mask, given its lack of a bodily anchor, yet the face claims individuality and a naturalistic look.[50] One may read this drawing as participating in notions of African and African American primitivism; the wild hair and the name "Congo" create the sense that this is a wild ani-mal on exhibit, a Noble Savage presented to the American reader. On the other hand, this drawing is nothing like the stereotypes of the Mammy or Uncle Tom sort.

The next six drawings are full portraits of the sitters.[51] Each depicts a figure (or two—a mother and child are the subjects of one drawing) dressed in light-colored clothing. The portraits are serious, even somber images that allude to the interior life of the individual. The expressions on the faces are neither happy nor sad; the "types" seem wrapped in thought.[52] The sitters are not identified by name, and so the viewer does not receive any biographical information. Rather, the captions emphasize typifying characteristics: *Mother and Child, Young America: Native-Born, A College Lad*. Other conventional means of identifying individuals in portraits, such as clothing, do situate the subjects somewhat. One caption

Figure 12. Winold Reiss, *Congo: A Familiar of New York Studios*. Illustration for *Survey Graphic*, March 1925. Republished 1979; reproduced by permission of Black Classic Press. Courtesy of Fisk University Galleries, Nashville, Tenn.

identifies the sitter as *Girl in the White Blouse*.[53] The captions and clothing point to the many roles African Americans can occupy, but emphasize "type" rather than a unique individual or stereotype.

The manner in which the clothing was drawn reveals Reiss's use of a design-centered, experimental idiom. Each drawing is a study of shape, line, and tone as much as it is a study of a type. In *Young America* and *A Boy Scout* especially, Reiss eliminates much of the detail of the clothing, creating a contrast between the realistic face and the patterns in the cloth. Reiss may have developed this style as a consequence of working with von Stuck in Germany. Von Stuck placed onionskin on top of photographs, which he then traced. These tracings served as the basis for his painted portraits. In fact, von Stuck's most famous work, *Die Sünde* (The Sin; 1895), portrays the light-colored body of a woman emerging from a dark field of color, thereby contrasting the realistically rendered torso with the indeterminate shapes of the background, and with the gilt frame created by the artist himself.[54] One can imagine that Reiss's technique—combining almost photographic facial style with outlined clothing and blank background—developed from work that blended contrasts in color, shape, and precision with the interest in social position and ethnography that was characteristic of the Neue Sachlichkeit. Indeed, Locke saw this as an example of "modernistic technique."[55]

Reiss's final drawing, *A College Lad* (Figure 13), segues into Du Bois's essay "The Black Man Brings His Gifts." *A College Lad* is larger than the previous drawings, except for *Congo*. It depicts a young black man dressed in a suit, with a watch chain in his vest. The clothing is done in outline, and the face is naturalistically rendered. This drawing is much more flattering than the previous drawings. It emphasizes the external markers of social status and the interior life of the young man, together culminating in the development of the New Negro.[56] In fact, the choice of *Congo* and *A College Lad* to frame the other types was not accidental. *Survey Graphic*'s associate editor, Sara Merrill, wrote to Locke: "I think the series accomplishes a definite purpose as it stands. The college lad is the type farthest removed from the man from the Congo, . . . a wide span between the two."[57] Each of the portraits presents a type, along a continuum of black identity. Yet the figures possess interior lives and are depicted as more complex than stereotypes. In sum, Reiss presents drawings that negotiate the boundaries between type and individual identity. Given the context of the pieces (the captions and the clothing, which veers away from realist renderings to abstract design, as well as the order in which they are presented), Reiss accentuates their typical and even, perhaps, stereotypical characteristics.

With its essays and images, the *Survey Graphic* had a clearly established means of representing types, a mechanism—documentation of types in word and image—that it turned on the New Negroes emerging from the Great Migration. Locke, however, seemed to find the patterns of the magazine constricting. Perhaps he found its bias toward the documentary and its claims of accuracy limited, not "new" enough to get at the core of the New Negro, the "common condition" and "consciousness" of a race.[58] Throughout the magazine, fissures emerge precisely where Locke's editorial hand is evident. These are fault lines between the *Survey*'s standard

Figure 13. Winold Reiss, *A College Lad*. Illustration for *Survey Graphic,* March 1925. Re-published 1979; reproduced by permission of Black Classic Press. Courtesy of the Mitchell Wolfson Jr. Collection, Wolfsonian-Florida International University, Miami Beach, Florida.

formula and claims of veracity and Locke's insistence on diversifying representations to challenge Old Negro representations and include New Negro representations, especially in the realm of arts and letters. Ultimately, Locke would include more examples of a "serious and careful realism" and "modernist art" in the anthology, thereby broadening the manner in which African Americans were portrayed.[59]

The issue's index and opening comments (written by Joseph K. Hart, an editor of the magazine) are the first indication that Locke was pushing against the preestablished form of the survey. They are at odds with the table of contents of the material gathered and arranged by Locke. In his opening essay "What Shall We Do with the Facts?" Hart stresses the supremacy of the "fact"-based agenda of the magazine over its more subjective, aesthetically concerned aspects. Seventeen of the eighteen categories (used in all issues of the *Survey Graphic*) found in the index are concerned with social issues, such as "child welfare," "mental hygiene," "education outside the school," and "conquest of disease." Only the last category of the index, "motives and ideals," has concerns that are more esoteric. Even the poetry that occupies almost four full pages falls under the category "immigration and race relations" and is labeled as relating to "youth and the race." In addition, the Langston Hughes poem "Our Land," the Reiss drawings that accompany the poem, and three modernist Reiss images illustrating an article entitled "Jazz at Home" are omitted from the index. By relegating poetry to its sociological content and using editorial tactics that seek to erase the presence of material, the editors presented the magazine purely as a vehicle for articles of social interest and social work.

Locke, on the other hand, stressed his own agenda, revealing his ambivalence about the magazine's sociological approach. The first section, entitled "The Greatest Negro Community in the World," focuses on the social conditions of Negro life in Harlem, with illustrative material. The second section, "The Negro Expresses Himself," addresses questions of representing the emotional, personal, and individual lives of New Negroes. The third section, "Black and White—Studies in Race Contacts," deals with a variety of social issues and their effects on African American "types."

The pattern of organization of the issue stresses both a sociological depiction of Harlem and a more self-reflexive artistic interpretation of African America. Moreover, it places the community in a context that takes into account the relations between black and white. Both are aims that Locke made explicit in "Enter the New Negro." This has the effect of emphasizing the distinctive temper of Harlem, both as a community and as a field of artistic expression within a larger American context.

Locke's simultaneously sociological and psychological project shaped the magazine and the visual and textual materials it offered. Many of the drawings, photographs, and articles employ mimetic and naturalistic forms. With these sorts of images and text, the magazine could discuss, for example, the "black worker," the church, or the pattern of Harlem's settlement. But Locke, in "Enter the New Negro," had criticized the limitations of "the watch and guard of statistics" employed by "the Sociologist, the Philanthropist, the Race Leader." They could not "account" for the New Negro, since (Locke seemed to conclude) the tyranny of statistics was as bad as the tyranny of stereotypes.[60]

The cover of the *Survey Graphic* calls attention to the complex dance between type and individual, social science or journalistic and aesthetic readings of the modern African American experience, and a realist visual discourse and a modernist idiom, which Locke later defined as "art with the shorthand emphasis on generalized forms rather than pictorial realism or photographic detail."[61] The cover (Figure 14) presents a drawing of Roland Hayes by Reiss, framed by the name of the magazine and blue Art Deco designs, which epitomize Locke's resistance to the documentary and illustrative idiom employed by the magazine.

The portrait is an almost photographic view of the singer, who was a master of the German lieder. His head floats on the cover, anchored neither by body nor by background. The designs, which border it on the left and right, evoke the machines of the industrial age: triangles and wheels with spokes. The lack of any identifying context is significant; there is no body to anchor the head, literally or figuratively, in a naturalistic tradition. The juxtaposition of a quasi-realistic portrait with design calls attention to the tension between what Locke called "pictorial realism" and "modernism or abstract art."[62]

With the head as the focal point of the cover, Hayes comes to be associated more with the words directly underneath him, "Harlem: Mecca of the New Negro," rather than with the words to the right: "Roland Hayes, Drawn by Winold Reiss."[63] The effect of this is to stress that this man possesses a complex identity. He is the epitome of changes wrought by the urbanization of the African American population, a typical and representative New Negro, and an individual, though notably one without a body.

This drawing is reprinted opposite Locke's opening article, entitled "Harlem." In this reproduction, a caption follows the name "Roland Hayes": "Whose achievement as a singer symbolized the promise of the younger generation."[64] Despite Reiss's design, the portrait of Hayes emphasizes the singer as a representative New Negro. He is marshaled as a

Figure 14. Winold Reiss, *Roland Hayes*. Cover illustration for *Survey Graphic*, March 1925.
Republished 1979; reproduced by permission of Black Classic Press.

representative of a specific generation of blacks in America, rather than as
a nameless but typical member of a mass.

The *Survey Graphic* literature likewise straddles the traditional and the
modern. Locke included a number of poems in the issue. Claude McKay's
three poems are in sonnet form, with regular rhyme scheme and meter.

Two poems, "Strong Tree" and "Russian Cathedral," avoid issues overtly related to race, while a third, "White Houses," is about the rage a black man feels in the United States and his attempt to quell that anger in order to fit into American society. The poem addresses both a white reader (or perhaps American society in general) and the black man himself:

> Oh, I must search for wisdom every hour,
> Deep in my wrathful bosom sore and raw,
> And find in it the superhuman power
> To hold me to the letter of your law![65]

The poem, though composed in regular meter and rhyme, describes a profound anger and discontent. The hate the man feels in his "wrathful bosom" is palpable; it emerges in a description of his tightened face. Although the classical form of the poem—it is a sonnet—tempers the condemnation of and disappointment in the "letter of your law," the disgust for the inequities of the United States is forceful. The title had originally been "The White House."[66] The change both enlarges the scope of the poem and diminishes its anger. The plural form makes the houses nonspecific—no longer referring to the capital—and nonrepresentative.

The poetry of Langston Hughes, in contrast, does not register in the same range. The poems that appeared in the magazine ("Dream Variation," "The Dream Keeper," and "Jazzonia") celebrate black life, using colloquialisms and everyday images. "Jazzonia" accompanies J. A. Rogers' essay "Jazz at Home" and Reiss's two drawings (*Interpretations of Harlem Jazz*), which are abstract, collage-like works—charcoal sketches in black, white, and gray.[67] They portray jazz with references to skyscrapers and smokestacks—the visual landscape of modern life. People in sophisticated suits or evening dresses dance, talk, and play. The drawings echo the urban, modern feel of the essay and poem.

In short, throughout the *Survey Graphic,* the literature, essays, and art formulated a tension between realistic and modernistic forms and between the sociological or documentary approaches and the interest in *belles-lettres.* The effect was to gather an enormous amount of attention not only for the New Negroes but also for their work. Locke's interartistic collection proved hugely successful and set in motion the rest of his endeavors.

To the New Negro: An Interpretation

Noting the tremendous interest in the upcoming New Negro issue of the *Survey Graphic,* Albert Boni approached Paul Kellogg early in 1925 with the idea of transforming the magazine into a book-length anthology.[68] Boni conceived of shifting the work into a "much more formidable volume," with the scope "not Harlem, but the cultural revival as a whole."[69] In a letter of March 17, 1925, he confirmed Locke's editorship.[70] Eight months later, in November, Boni published a book version of the magazine (it was reprinted in 1927).[71]

When Locke revised the *Survey Graphic* for the first printing of *The New Negro,* he changed not only the local focus but also the relationship between the textual and the visual. The guiding principle of the interartistic in the *Survey Graphic* is documentary of social facts, with visual images used to illustrate the claims of articles and independent visual images used as evidence of the magazine's claims about types. In many respects, the anthology is a simpler work. It does not interweave the textual and the visual on the page or employ the visual as supporting and subordinate illustration. The interartistic scheme of the anthology juxtaposes word and image as equivalent creative expressions about the New Negro, and ultimately *by* the New Negro.

Locke accomplishes this in part by bringing together writing from all sectors of New Negro literary life. The contents include "Negro Art and America," "The Negro in American Literature," "Negro Youth Speaks: Fiction, Poetry, Drama, Music," "The Negro Digs Up His Past." The second section of the contents echoes some of the social interest of the *Survey* ("The New Scene: Harlem—the Culture Capital," "Howard: The National Negro University," "The Negro's Americanism," "The Paradox of Color"), and indeed some of the articles are identical to those in the magazine. In no way, however, do the *Survey Graphic*'s social concerns dominate the anthology.

The design of the book calls attention to the creative accomplishments of the New Negro and to individual New Negroes. Reiss's contributions consist of portraits and decorations, placed at the beginning or end of the literary pieces and essays. Reiss employed an Art Deco, black-and-white style, similar to that of some of the images he had published in the *Survey Graphic.* At times, the decorations include masks, referring perhaps to the African masks whose photos appear in the anthology; at other times, they are abstract designs.[72] Reiss uses black-and-white design, with hard lines. Locke's essay "The New Negro," for example, is bordered by a mask, set amid a black-and-white pattern. Reiss's portraits, half of a series he did of New Negroes, are presented in full-color plates; scattered throughout the text, they are printed separately on glossy paper.[73] The presentation of the portraits suggests that they are worth preserving—indeed, collector's items.[74]

Although Locke included poetry, drama, and short stories of all sorts in the anthology, he makes his clearest attempt to complicate the racial representation in the magazine through the introduction of new elements, especially a vigorous realism that departed from *Survey* types and modernist work that was connected to African America. He accomplished this first by moving away from "types" to "representatives," and second by including the work of African American visual artist Aaron Douglas.

Locke expanded the subjects of Reiss's types from the *Survey Graphic* to include representative portrayals of the elite of Harlem's intelligentsia. Portraits of authors, in full color, accompany articles the authors wrote. Locke included only one of Reiss's "phantasies"—abstract drawings that were meant to evoke or interpret jazz. He reluctantly added some work by the Mexican caricaturist Miguel Covarrubias, whose drawings cannot claim figurative resemblance in the same way that Reiss's do, for he often used techniques of caricature found in other publications of that era.[75] And Locke gladly included modernist drawings by Douglas, those concerned with design, shape, and contrast.

Locke was convinced of the transformative power of Reiss's portraits.[76] Yet he and Reiss no longer wanted types. Instead, they called for "representatives"—clearly recognizable, verifiable, and (most important) public figures.[77] On February 18, 1925, Charles S. Johnson wrote to Locke that Reiss was interested in having Locke sit for him. "His interests have grown to include persons who are a bit more than types—he wants representatives now. Mr. Reiss has asked me to complete the group. I think you ought to be in the series by all means."[78] The fact that Reiss did a portrait of Locke (Figure 15), a clearly recognizable, well-known, and significant individual, and wanted to do portraits of other New Negroes, including Jean Toomer, Countee Cullen, and Paul Robeson, suggests the extent to which representatives were winning out over types as foundational to the aesthetic logic of the book.

Locke probably recognized the danger that types posed, for the transition to stereotype could be made quickly. His turn from types to the inclusion of representatives or "individuals, not mere types," suggests a desire to expand beyond the images used as evidence for sociological claims or journalistic observations to include a range of images, including portraits of recognizable and unique individuals.[79] The effect of these representatives is to expand ideas of the New Negroes, to convey the achievement of veritable Harlem Renaissance participants as individual black men and women, rather than as generic types of African Americans.

The inclusion of representatives may have had something to do with the controversy that the Reiss drawings had caused at a public meeting in Har-

Figure 15. Winold Reiss, *Alain Locke*. Illustration for *The New Negro: An Interpretation*, 1925. Courtesy of the National Portrait Gallery, Smithsonian Institution; gift of Lawrence A. Fleischman and Howard Garfinkle with a matching grant from the National Endowment for the Arts.

lem. Shortly after the publication of the March 1925 *Survey Graphic,* a number of readers began to complain about Reiss's drawings, especially the one that depicted two schoolteachers (Figure 16). Elise Johnson McDougald, who sat for Reiss and whose portrait was placed next to her article "The Double Task" in the *Survey Graphic,* wrote to Locke about the "furore" that arose around the portraits.

> The other night at the Harlem Forum a lively discussion followed Mr. Kellogg's address. One Mr. Williams wondered if the whole art side of the issue were a "piece of subtle propaganda to prejudice the white reader." He told us that "Should he meet those two school teachers in the street, he would be afraid of them." It happened that one of them, Miss Price, had come in late with me from another meeting. When an opportune moment arrived, she stood to express her regret that she would frighten him but claimed the portrait as a "pretty good likeness."[80]

The contrast between the "pretty good likeness" and the "subtle propaganda" points to the shift from types to representatives ultimately embraced by Locke. A type, free of a clearly indicated antecedent, could be read as positive or negative propaganda, as a figure meant to stand for the mass of African Americans. "Mr. Williams" clearly preferred that a typical figure be positive and flattering, something Locke found absurd. Yet the fact that the portrait was of an actual individual, and in fact resembled that individual, counters that desire. The notion of "likeness," when claimed by the model for the drawing, supersedes any readings of the image as typical.

Soon after, Locke wrote "To Certain of Our Philistines," an essay about the public reaction to Reiss's work. In a state of indignation, he declared: "Too many of us still look to art to compensate the attitudes of prejudice, rather than merely, as is proper, to ignore them." He believed that art should do more than function as a corrective to prejudice; art that that was merely a corrective he labeled "propaganda," a matter about which he and Du Bois disagreed often and publicly. He wanted racial art to stand for nothing more than itself: "Unfortunately for art, the struggle for social justice has put a pessimism upon a playing-up to Caucasian type-ideals, and created too prevalently a half-caste psychology that distorts all true artistic values with the irrelevant social values of 'representative' and 'unrepresentative,' 'favorable' and 'unfavorable'—and threatens a truly racial art with the psychological bleach of 'lily-whitism.' This Philistinism cannot be tolerated."[81] Locke could not stomach the criticism Reiss's drawings received. It reflected an uneducated public, which accepted ideal notions of beauty

Figure 16. Winold Reiss, *Two Public School Teachers*. Illustration for *Survey Graphic,* March 1925. Republished 1979; reproduced by permission of Black Classic Press. Courtesy of Fisk University Galleries, Nashville, Tenn.

that were determined by Caucasian phenotypes and believed that representations of African Americans should aspire to those ideals at the expense of real and unique individuality. Locke called the drawing of the two schoolteachers "most realistic, . . . [with] sheer poetry and intense symbolism back of it," and "finely representative," thereby removing any possibility that it would become a stereotype.[82]

In many respects, the anthologies are the fulfillment of Locke's desire to counter the stereotypes of earlier representational forms by presenting the heterogeneity of the African American population. But the critics who published in the anthology had an additional agenda: they were intent on defining a new aesthetic for a uniquely African American identity—"a distinctively Negro art," as collector Albert Barnes put it.[83] Locke, for his part, celebrated what he saw as the unique modernity of the New Negro, as well as the "vigorous realism" and the "modernism," a sentiment in keeping with his earlier writings. In his introduction to the fiction and poetry, he wrote of "Negro youth": "It has been their achievement also to bring the artistic advance of the Negro sharply into stepping alignment with contemporary artistic thought, mood, and style. They are thoroughly modern, some of them ultra-modern, and Negro thoughts now wear the uniform of the age."[84] Their unique contribution was the "transfusion of racial idioms with the modernistic styles of expression."[85]

But some contention remained as to the source of this "distinctive" art. Barnes found its source in the Negro's "primitive nature" and his "emotional endowment, his luxuriant and free imagination and a truly great power of individual expression."[86] What can this "primitive" Negro best produce? Braithwaite had a very specific answer to this question: poetry, a literary form closely related to song. Barnes agreed: "The Negro is a poet by birth. . . . Poetry is religion brought down to earth and it is of the essence of the Negro soul. He carries it with him always and everywhere; he lives it in the field, the shop, the factory. His daily habits of thought, speech and movement are flavored with picturesque, the rhythmic, the euphonious."[87] Given this understanding of inherent Negro ability and talent for song, it is unsurprising that Braithwaite wrote: "The development of fiction among Negro authors has been, I might say, one of the repressed activities of our literary life."[88]

These are troubling assertions in the context of the material that Locke includes, since the focus on the unique and essential African American literary aesthetic reveals some of the biases and stereotypes associated with the Old Negro. For Barnes and Braithwaite (surprisingly, given Braithwaite's interest in combating stereotypes), the unique aesthetic sensibility was based on some inherent qualities of African American identity: a primitive constitution and a proximity to nature. Locke, however, did not want to accept that sentiment, because if these were not stereotypes of the Old Negro, then they certainly could become stereotypes of the New Negro, stereotypes that if not countered could become a "serious misrepresentation" akin to those of the nineteenth century.[89] "What we have thought primitive in the American Negro—his naïveté, his sentimentalism, his exuberance and his improvising spontaneity are then neither characteristically African nor to be explained as ancestral heritage. They are the result of his peculiar experience in America and the emotional upheaval of its trials and ordeals."[90] How was he to assert the New Negro aesthetic without resorting to stereotypes?

For Locke, the answer was the visual. By way of African art, African Americans could make a proprietary claim on a major inspiration for modern art. Locke's essay "The Legacy of the Ancestral Arts" and his later work *Negro Art: Past and Present* stressed the importance of the African plastic arts, "for contemporary European painting and sculpture just such a mine of fresh motifs."[91] Matisse, Picasso, Derain, Modigliani, and other stars of the modernist firmament were the models African American artists should emulate. "If African art is capable of producing the ferment in modern art that it has, surely this is not too much to expect of its influence upon the culturally awakened Negro artist of the present generation."[92]

In the "new artistic respect for the African idiom and the natural ambition of Negro artists for a racial idiom in their art expression," Locke found the most viable means of combating the "timid conventionalism" engendered by "racial disparagement."[93] In other words, the respect commanded by African art among modern artists and those who admired it would translate into respect for African American artists engaging with African forms and a sense of African heritage.[94] Moreover, African American visual artists could assert simultaneously the modernity, the modernism, and the Africanism of the New Negro.

The inclusion of work by Aaron Douglas and to a lesser degree the work of Reiss was the means by which Locke expanded the *Survey*'s conventions of racial representation to include a modern and modernist program. Reiss's decorations throughout the text as well as elements of his portraits push the boundaries of the realistic types demanded by the *Survey*. Indeed, Locke later described Reiss as a "realist" and referred to his "modernistic technique." But the inclusion of a large number of images by Douglas, whom Locke calls one of the "first converts" to modernism, expanded the boundaries of racial representation.[95]

Douglas had come across the New Negro issue of the *Survey Graphic* in his native Kansas City, where he was teaching art. He soon arrived in Harlem, where he stayed for years. The *Survey Graphic*, he later recalled, was "the most cogent single factor that eventually turned my face to New York."[96] Riveted by the power of the visual material that Locke had collected in the magazine, the young artist wrote to Locke. Not long afterward, the elder critic was literally knocking on his door.[97] Locke was impressed enough with Douglas' work to include six black-and-white drawings in the 1925 printing and eleven in the 1927 printing, in addition to the large number of works by the established artist Reiss.

Douglas was openly excited about providing work for the anthology. He admired Locke (though his admiration was somewhat qualified) and greatly respected Reiss and his work.[98] In addition, he was honored to be the sole African American visual artist included in *The New Negro*.[99]

Reiss influenced Douglas' contributions to the anthology and indeed to the Harlem Renaissance. Douglas had met Reiss through Charles S. Johnson in 1925, after which Reiss took the younger man under his wing and gave him a two-year scholarship for study.[100] Reiss's style transformed Douglas' work. After seeing the elder artist's work and meeting him, Douglas moved his work from conventional figurative drawing to a style that relied heavily on geometric shape and the contrast between black and white. Amy Kirschke has pointed to the possible influence of the *Scherenschnitt*, the German folk art of scissors-cut images, on Reiss.[101] Folk artists used black cutouts without depth or perspective, and Reiss employed a black-and-white form to evoke folklife. It is also possible that, aside from absorbing this technique from Reiss, Douglas used black-and-white silhouette tradition, and made it modern and African American by hardening the lines and referring to African sculpture.

Douglas and Reiss, however, worked in naturalistic as well as stylized modes, and their work exhibited some affinities. Both used Art Deco techniques for building and interior decorations. At that time, Douglas was decorating Club Ebony and Reiss was completing work on the Congo Room at the Hotel Almanac in New York.[102] Douglas and others recognized the similarities in their work. But he also saw differences, as he noted when he showed Reiss some of his work. He wrote in a letter that while Reiss's and his drawings had some superficial similarities, they were, in fact, quite different in style.[103]

Given that there were similarities between the work of the two artists, Locke had a choice to make: he could include the figurative work or abstract work of one and not the other, or he could include both types of work from each artist. Although there are representational and abstract images of both artists in the text, Locke chose to foreground Reiss's representative figures and Douglas' black-and-white, geometric designs. Perhaps this suggests an aesthetic divide between them that does not hold up when one looks at their larger oeuvres; more likely, this choice reflects some of the pressure to include work by an African American artist, who in this case produced modernist work that referred to African sculpture.[104] This change from the magazine suggests that Locke conceived of *The New Negro* not as a purely literary anthology but as an interartistic text whose final form was meant to depict black Americans from a variety of angles, including realistic portraits and a native African American modernism.

The choices that Locke made about the work of the two artists can best be apprehended by looking at two drawings bearing the same name that they each did for the anthology. Reiss and Douglas each published a drawing entitled *Ancestral* in the first printing of *The New Negro* (neither appeared in the *Survey Graphic*). Reiss's drawing (Figure 17), which is labeled a "type sketch," is a vivid color portrait of a seated woman dressed in brightly colored cloth. On her head she wears a long white shawl, which she gathers around her torso with her hands. Her clothing, in shades of orange and blue, peeks out from the shawl. The woman looks directly out of the frame, smiling. Her skintone is coffee, modulated with white to create the effect of light. Her hands are similar in color to her face; her hair, a very dark brown with light highlights, is parted in the center. Behind the figure is a multicolored cloth or blanket with an abstract design. The colors in the blanket form vivid stripes and triangular shapes.

On one level, this could be a portrait of an easily recognizable individual, although the sitter is unnamed. On the other hand (and this is perhaps the greatest gift of Reiss), the portrait calls attention to the manner in which color and design could represent African American identity. The blanket is a blanket, but it is also a study in stripes, triangles, and circles and in yellow, red, and purple. Reiss calls attention to color in the depiction of African American identity when he juxtaposes the carefully shaded and tinted hands with the white of the cloth. He uses an attention to color and design for figurative purposes. This image also complicates the notion of a unitary type, because it stresses the Native American or perhaps Mexican roots of African America, undermining notions of racial homogeneity.

Douglas' *Ancestral*, titled *Rebirth* for the second printing of *The New Negro*, is a complex black-and-white painting (Figure 18). The painting includes many images: two central figures, with head and body; a face in the upper right corner; a sun in the upper left corner; and what appear to be

Figure 17. Winold Reiss, *Ancestral*. Illustration for Alain Locke, *The New Negro: An Interpretation*, 1925. Courtesy of Fisk University Galleries, Nashville, Tenn.

Figure 18. Aaron Douglas, *Ancestral*. Illustration for Alain Locke, *The New Negro: An Interpretation*, 1925. The Alta Sawyer and Aaron Douglas Foundation.

masks, faces, eyes, and other suns woven throughout the picture plane. Douglas views his subjects from many angles and creates a collage-like effect with the blocks of black and white.[105]

The drawing is composed of flat black-and-white shapes that form figures. There is little perspective, as the shapes stay on the surface of the picture plane. The figures are stylized. Unrecognizable in contrast to the figure in Reiss's *Ancestral,* they gain their human form through the opposition between black and white and through Douglas' lines, which tend to be hard and straight, rather than curvilinear. The figures thus take on the appearance of hard silhouettes. Like Reiss, Douglas pays attention both to figure and to design, avoiding pure abstraction. Moreover, with his attention to the mask, Douglas refers to a generalized conception of Africa.

The differences between the two works are striking. Reiss's *Ancestral* connotes the ancestral through a naturalistic image, albeit framed by experiments in color and design. Douglas' work connotes the ancestral through shape, design, and blocks of black and white. The presence of both images in the single text suggests that Locke was aiming to expand New Negro representations in multiple directions, so long as these representations did not veer toward the stereotypical.

To the New Negro: An Interpretation, Number Two

The similarities between the first and second printings of *The New Negro* point to the consistency of Locke's vision of what a *belles-lettres* anthology of Harlem Renaissance should be. Locke maintained the form of the volume to a remarkable degree. For the second version, Locke paid even greater attention to the physical appearance of the book. He focused on the paper and the cardboard, writing to the publisher in detail about the "ivory tint or softer finish plate paper for softer values of color plates."[106] With an almost fastidious attention to detail, he attempted to construct an even more beautiful volume.

In the new version, Locke included five additional Douglas pieces: *The Emperor Jones, The Spirit of Africa, Roll, Jordan, Roll* (Figure 19), *And the Stars Began to Fall,* and *From the New World.* Some of these appeared as illustrations for the 1925 issue of *Opportunity,* which included Locke's article "The Technical Study of the Spirituals: A Review" and Arthur Fauset's article "The Negro's Cycle of Song: A Review."[107] Each of the drawings (except for *The Emperor Jones*) bears the name of a spiritual, and includes some reference to it. Douglas employs a crisp, hard line. The black-and-white of each drawing is stark; there is no gray anywhere. The

Figure 19. Aaron Douglas, *Roll, Jordan, Roll*. Illustration for Alain Locke, *The New Negro: An Interpretation*, 1927. The Alta Sawyer and Aaron Douglas Foundation.

effect is very much a silhouette style, almost as though Douglas had done the drawing out of black-and-white paper cutouts. That these images refer to spirituals suggests that Locke was adding elements to the anthology that would further open up ideas of the New Negro—to include thoughts on folk music, spirituality, and Southern life with a modernist idiom.

When Locke added the Douglas drawings to the material originally published in the *Survey Graphic,* the net effect was an explicit expansion of earlier representational forms, and a commitment to include what he considered an African American modernism along with realist work that moved beyond stereotypes and types.

While other 1920s magazines such as the *Crisis, Opportunity,* and *Vanity Fair* employed text and image to explore issues relating to black America, the overt agenda of the *Survey Graphic* and the two printings of *The New Negro* was representation of the New Negro, both as new types of African Americans and as a new sort of representation. By employing the textual and the visual, the magazine and the two printings of the anthology experimented with a number of racial aesthetics that addressed the character of racial identity and interrogated modern art's ability to portray blackness. In the works that Locke edited, he introduced the New Negro—the modern, urban African American of the 1920s. In his capacity as editor, first of a magazine and then of an anthology, he approached the New Negro from a number of different conceptual angles with a number of different aesthetic tools. Moreover, he was testing the racial aesthetics employed by his writers and artists. By placing so many different essays, poems, short stories, drawings, prints, and photographs together, in a series of volumes, Locke created a field in which he and his readers could use a variety of aesthetic styles and forms to account for the heterogeneity of the African American population, something denied by the stereotypes of the past.

chapter three

Fy-ah

SHORTLY AFTER THE PUBLICATION of the first printing of *The New Negro: An Interpretation,* W. E. B. Du Bois, perhaps the most prominent African American intellectual of the twentieth century, sponsored a symposium entitled "The Negro in Art: How Shall He Be Portrayed?" From February to November 1926, *The Crisis: A Record of the Darker Races,* the magazine Du Bois edited for the National Association for the Advancement of Colored People, published a series of responses to a questionnaire he had written. "There has long been controversy within and without the Negro race," he stated, "as to just how the Negro should be treated in art—how he should be pictured by writers and portrayed by artists." Du Bois wanted to know how artists, writers, publishers, and audiences balanced the demands of "true" and "artistic" portrayals with the dangers of "the popular trend in portraying Negro character in the underworld."[1]

Du Bois, then fifty-eight, was a Harvard-educated and European-trained intellectual with Victorian sensibilities. He sent his questionnaire to a variety of individuals—whites and blacks, authors and publishers, critics and artists, young and old. Among the respondents were controversial writer Carl Van Vechten, young poet Langston Hughes, fellow *Crisis* editor Jessie Fauset, Pulitzer Prize–winning Southern writer Julia Peterkin, publisher Alfred Knopf, and elder black writer Charles Chesnutt. Du Bois asked seven questions about issues of representation, publication, and dissemination. He inquired about the obligations or limitations of artists in portraying African Americans and asked whether it was appropriate to criticize publishers or authors for their depictions. He solicited views on the tendency of authors to portray the worst sort of blacks and on the dangers facing young artists in the contemporary art environment. In general, he wanted each respondent to imagine a program for African American literature and art.

Although the symposium had a question-and-answer format, the inquiries seem structured to elicit certain responses; Du Bois seemed to have had answers in mind when he wrote his queries. Like Benjamin Brawley, William Stanley Braithwaite and others, he saw a danger in white representations that fixed blacks into stereotypes, but he also saw a danger emerging from within the black community itself.[2] He decried the tendency of writers to portray a specific "type" of Negro, and the propensity of publishers to encourage such portrayals. The type to which Du Bois referred was the "sordid, foolish, and criminal" Negro. The problem was that the type could come to stand for all Negroes rather than "the best characters" of American blacks.[3]

The range of the responses published in the *Crisis* was broad. Some critics followed Du Bois; Brawley, for example, thought that the portrayals of the "worst" were harmful. Others, such as Van Vechten and Knopf, thought that all portrayals were necessary. Peterkin admired the "Black Negro Mammy" type, while Chesnutt wanted writers and artists to create ideals. Hughes wrote a short, five-sentence answer: "What's the use of saying anything—the true literary artist is going to write about what he chooses anyway, regardless of outside opinions."[4]

The symposium reflects both the importance of periodicals for the Harlem Renaissance and the debates about racial representation. Magazines constituted a major source of publicity for African American writers and artists, and an important forum for their work.[5] The *Crisis* and *Opportunity: Journal of Negro Life* (the latter had emerged from the National Urban League) sponsored literary contests to encourage and publish young writers. Charles S. Johnson, editor of *Opportunity*, declared that the aim of these contests was "to stimulate creative literary effort among Negroes; to locate and orient Negro writers of ability; to stimulate and encourage interest in the serious developments of a body of literature about Negro life." Johnson's commercial goals were explicit: he wanted "to foster a market for Negro writers and for literature by and about Negroes."[6]

Writers, publishers, and others also used these magazines—in addition to periodicals owned and operated by non–African Americans—as sites for debates. They argued, in print, about politics and culture, especially about art and propaganda in the field of African American arts and letters. Although his position varied throughout the 1910s and 1920s, by 1926 Du Bois was claiming that that "all Art is Propaganda and ever must be, despite the wailing of the purists."[7] Johnson, in *Opportunity*, was more circumspect, arguing for the freedom of writers and artists while recognizing the social import of art.[8] Other writers wrestled with the same issue, including Alain Locke, who would later publish an article entitled "Art and Propaganda."

In 1925, a young man of twenty-three arrived in Harlem ready to take on these magazines, which he believed were entrenched in the politics of their organizations and in outdated aesthetic positions. His name was Wallace Thurman and he had come from Los Angeles. Langston Hughes described him as a "strangely brilliant black boy, who had read everything, and whose critical mind could find something wrong with everything he read."[9] In L.A. he had edited a magazine called the *Outlet,* which was his attempt to create a New Negro movement in California.[10] In Harlem, he worked at the *Looking Glass* and the *World Tomorrow,* a white-owned magazine. He served briefly as an editor at the *Messenger,* in which he published a number of articles that placed him squarely in opposition to Du Bois by rejecting books that were clearly in the "propagandist school."[11]

Less than a year after his arrival, Thurman was associating with a wide swath of young Harlem Renaissance writers, artists, actors, and musicians. In the "sweltering summer" of 1926, Thurman and writer Gwendolyn Bennett, Harvard Law student John Davis, Langston Hughes, Columbia-trained anthropologist Zora Neale Hurston, and Richard Bruce Nugent—a writer and artist who was in the habit of walking around Harlem in his bare feet—gathered at Aaron Douglas' apartment. There, they discussed a new publishing venture that would break with the established magazines and with the elders of the Harlem Renaissance. They conceived of *Fire!!*—a small and ultimately short-lived fine-arts magazine, similar to other little magazines of the era, such as *Broom, Blast,* and *Poetry*.[12] In a review, Locke aptly described their efforts: "In *Fire,* a new quarterly 'devoted to younger Negro artists,' the youth section of the New Negro movement has marched off in a gay and self-confident manoeuvre of artistic secession."[13] As the rhetoric of artistic "secession"—which places *Fire!!* in the tradition of European secessions of the late nineteenth and early twentieth centuries—and the reference to youth suggest, *Fire!!* self-consciously broke from the African American arts and letters and the extant periodicals of the Harlem Renaissance.[14] It became a place where young writers and artists, while articulating a generational difference from their elders, didn't have to worry about propaganda. *Fire!!* was a venue for new New Negroes to publish what Locke described as "left-wing literary modernism with deliberate intent," work that was both thematically daring and formally experimental.[15]

But *Fire!!* was a commercial failure, and Thurman brought out another magazine, *Harlem,* in November 1928. Although a number of editors from *Fire!!* contributed to the new magazine, *Harlem*'s articles seemed different from those of *Fire!!*—more politically oriented and commercially viable. And the magazine had quite a different look; it seemed to have more in common with the *Crisis* and *Opportunity* than with *Fire!!* Yet despite the magazine's new design and the addition of a wider variety of articles, stories, advertisements, and other material, Thurman and his peers maintained their interest in themes and literary and artistic forms that the elders of the Harlem Renaissance considered inappropriate and, in some cases, shocking. This move suggests that Thurman was attempting to make his expansive approach to art and his interest in modernist experimentation more palatable and affordable to a wider audience. If *Fire!!* had been the younger generation's clear challenge to the strictures of elder New Negroes, *Harlem* was a subtle flouting of conventions without the requisite generational rhetoric.

Although *Fire!!* had been very much a collaboration among the six founders, Thurman was the one who articulated the clearest program for the magazines and for his peers. During the 1920s, he reflected on the state of magazine publishing and on the status of African American arts and letters. In a number of articles, published in the *New Republic, Messenger,* and his own magazines, Thurman elaborated on his differences from older journalists, who, he believed, had focused too much on politics and problems—"spouting fire and venom or else weeping and moaning."[16] The tendency of black journalists to accuse white people of being "dastards, in denying him [the Negro] equal economic opportunities or in lynching him upon the slightest provocation," and their tendency to focus on "his own problem here in America," may have been appropriate in an earlier era, but Thurman felt that this attitude was no longer effective or useful. Journalists had failed to respond to the changes wrought by the urbanization, industrialization, and modernization of the 1920s. They were "ludicrously out of tune with the other instruments in their environment."[17]

The "so-called negro art 'renaissance,'" as Thurman called it, was limited because commitment to racial progress had been allowed to trump literary standards. "Speaking purely of the arts," Thurman wrote, "the results of the renaissance have been sad rather than satisfactory, in that critical standards have been ignored, and the measure of achievement has been racial rather than literary."[18] When periodicals did expand their content to include "new voices" or "folk art" amid the "propaganda," they failed to do these voices justice. "But the artist was not satisfied to be squeezed between jeremiads or have his work thrown haphazardly upon a page where there was no effort to make it look beautiful as well as sound beautiful. He revolted against shoddy and sloppy publication methods, revolted against the patronizing attitudes his elders assumed toward him, revolted against their editorial astigmatism and their intolerance of new points of view."[19] Thurman saw a problem with both the editorial agendas and the physical aspect of the magazines. Editors and journalists—Thurman's "elders"—did not know yet how to deal with new artistic production. Resistant to innovation and change, they published with no eye for beauty and no ear for lyricism—qualities that were missing from propaganda.

The problem, Thurman suggested, lay not only with the magazines but also with much of contemporary African American arts and letters. Although he had difficulties with representations of the past, and condemned the Old Negroes just as elder critics such as Brawley, Braithwaite, and Locke had, he also rejected some contemporary representations, in effect articulating a generational difference between him and the older, more established writers and artists. In an editorial written for the *New Republic* in 1927, Thurman condemned the tendency of some African American writers and artists to offer hackneyed and sugarcoated portrayals. "The American Negro feels that he has been misinterpreted and caricatured so long by insincere artists that once a Negro gains the ear of the public he should expend his spiritual energy feeding the public honeyed manna on a silver spoon." The public too was to blame, for they were unable to distinguish between stereotype and quality: "They seem unable to fathom the innate difference between a dialect farce committed by an Octavus Roy Cohen to increase the gaiety of Babbitts, and a dialect interpretation done by a Negro writer to express some abstract something that burns within his people and sears him." The public created an atmosphere such that "Negroes in America feel they must always exhibit specimens from the college rather than from the kindergarten, specimens from the parlor rather than from the pantry."[20] Thurman was referring, perhaps, to the "college lad" of the *Survey Graphic* (Reiss's type sketch celebrated by Locke) or to the photographs of African American achievers that appeared in the *Crisis*. Challenging his elders, Thurman believed that art and literature that portrayed only "proper" African American identity, palatable to a middle-class audience, were unacceptable.

This contemporary problem—of limiting African Americans to portrayals of the "butter side up," as Thurman wrote—was as bad as the problem of limiting African Americans to the stereotypes of the past.[21] In a comment on Van Vechten's *Nigger Heaven,* Thurman made this connection explicit:

> Why Negroes imagine that any writer is going to write what Negroes think he ought to write about them is too ridiculous to merit consideration. It would seem that they would shy away from being pigeon-holed, so long have they been the rather lamentable victims of such a typically American practice, yet Negroes would have all Negroes appearing in contemporary literature made as ridiculous and as false to type as the older school of pseudo-humorous, sentimental white writers made their Uncle Toms, their Topsys, and their Mammies, or as the Octavus Roy Cohen school now make their more modern "cullud" folk.[22]

Thurman thus saw two difficulties for African American arts and letters: public, middle-class African Americans (whites of a darker hue, Thurman thought) wanted clean, benign images that ignored other members of the African American population, and Negro artists and writers gave such images to the public. The solution he called for was not only a broader representation of African Americans of all sorts, especially of the working class, but a change in artists themselves: art was to be produced by blacks who did not abide by the conventions of white America. He wanted his peers to create representations that were true to themselves and their own experience, and not to the imagined Negro of whites and certain sectors of black America. Thurman demanded a "truly Negroid note" in the American canon, by which he meant a body of African American art and literature that not only was created by blacks but reflected the range of African American experiences. These experiences would include representations of the "proletariat rather than the bourgeoisie, . . . people who still retained some individual race qualities and who were not totally white American in every respect save color of skin."[23]

Thurman cast *Fire!!* as a new attempt to satisfy the material and aesthetic concerns of the Harlem Renaissance writers and artists. It was a "new type of journal," an "independent art magazine" that would offer image and text, beautifully presented and representative of the range of the African American population. It would make editorial decisions that were different from those of other magazines and would publish literary and visual work that expanded the subject matter and form of earlier and current work.[24]

In many respects, *Fire!!* was the fulfillment of Thurman's goals. It was a wholly black-produced magazine. The contributors were iconoclastic black bohemians, experimenting with alternatives to the Victorian sensibilities of the old guard and the representational parameters of the elders of the Harlem Renaissance. The art and literature employed experimental literary and artistic forms—playing with language, narrative, shape, and design, as in "the bold, arresting red and black of its jacket"[25]—that dealt with taboo subjects (sexuality, prostitution, drug use, the working class) and that may have shocked both the "better class of colored people" and a generation older by only a few years.

Aaron Douglas wrote a manifesto for the group in which he set out the its identity and agenda:[26] "We are all under thirty. We have no get-rich-quick complex. We espouse no new theories of racial advancement, socially, economically, or politically. We have no axes to grind. We are group conscious. We are primarily and intensely devoted to art."[27] Douglas' language—the repetition of "we" and the explicit statements in the manifesto—reveals a profound sense of group consciousness, of youth, and of the group's sense of difference from their African American elders and from whites. The contributors to *Fire!!* were anticommercial; they believed that if African American art was to avoid being inherently exploitative, it had to be indigenously produced and economically supported by the African American community. The manifesto was an exceptionally strong and overt demand for African American artists and writers to engage in black image-making for an African American audience and to move away from the propaganda of some Harlem Renaissance magazines edited by their elders.

If part of the coterie's agenda was the rejection of the strategies of their elders, alluded to in "theories of racial advancement, socially, economically, or politically," then another aim was the reworking of the physical aspect of the magazine. The editors of *Fire!!* paid a great deal of attention to its appearance, including the artwork and the manner in which articles, stories, and poems appeared on the page. Douglas' cover, which Locke noted, a study of Egyptian and African motifs in black and red, is an optical illusion of a sort (Figure 20). At first glance, it is dominated by a sphinx-like figure in profile, surrounded by abstract shapes. At second glance, the abstract shapes coalesce into a profile: an ear with earring occupies the right side, while an eye, nose, and mouth occupy the left. The title

Figure 20. Aaron Douglas, Cover illustration for *Fire!!* 1926. The Alta Sawyer and Aaron Douglas Foundation.

Fire!! is done in Art Deco block letters. Underneath, in a similar font, are the words *Devoted to Younger Negro Artists.* The cover looks more like a work of art than a mere medium for conveying information about price and publication, for in no way does it call attention to itself as a commercial enterprise: it shows neither a price nor a volume number. On the whole, the images on the cover call attention to abstract design, contrast, and color, while remaining concerned with the representational.

The remainder of the magazine displays individual pieces of art and literature. Poems appear on the page like paintings in a frame. The section "Flame from the Dark Tower" includes ten poems, each printed in italics, centered on the page and framed by a pair of wavy black lines. This layout, quite different from that of the *Survey Graphic* or the *Crisis,* suggests that the poems are aesthetic objects in and of themselves. In *Fire!!,* the appearance of the poems seems as important as the poems themselves, clearly earmarking it as a fine-arts magazine.

Like the "Flame from the Dark Tower" poetry series, each drawing in *Fire!!* occupies an entire page. A page with the title "Three Drawings" precedes three images by Douglas, which do not serve as illustrations for any literary material in the text. Instead, their presentation makes them equivalent in importance to the literary works—an approach similar to that of *The New Negro.*

A striking aspect of *Fire!!* is that there are only two advertisements in the entire publication, and these serve an intellectual as well as commercial purpose. The ads, placed on the inside covers, are subscription forms for two other publications, the *New Masses* and *Opportunity.* The body of the magazine has no advertisements whatsoever. Compared to the many advertisements (for insurance, beauty products, books, and so on) that filled the pages of the other magazines of the time, the lack of attention to commercial enterprise is notable, suggesting a willful disregard of the business side of publication and an explicit commitment to creating a visually beautiful magazine.

If we consider the physical appearance of the magazine in total, rather than the literary and visual works in isolation, we gain an immediate sense of what the younger generation was after. The material aspect of *Fire!!*— the attention to typography, layout, and design—suggests an embrace of arts and letters as aesthetic objects, rather than an investment in explicitly commercial, social, or political concerns. Moreover, the relation between word and image intimates that both media are equivalent partners in the dissemination of the younger generation's aesthetics.

Yet we must turn to the themes and the forms of the material presented in *Fire!!* to understand how this self-consciously identified younger generation conceived of its aesthetic stance. The foreword to *Fire!!* set a combative tone for the magazine, one that both constructed a generational difference between the Thurman camp and the elders of the Harlem Renaissance and formulated an African American modernism:

> Fire . . . flaming, burning, searing, and penetrating far beneath the superficial items of the flesh to boil the sluggish blood.
> Fire . . . a cry of conquest in the night, warning those who sleep and revitalizing those who linger in the quiet places dozing.
> Fire . . . melting steel and iron bars, poking livid tongues between stone apertures and burning wooden opposition with cackling chuckle of contempt.
> Fire . . . weaving vivid, hot designs upon an ebon bordered loom and satisfying pagan thirst for beauty unadorned . . . the flesh is sweet and real . . . the soul an inward flush of fire . . . Beauty? . . . flesh on fire—on fire in the furnace of life blazing. . . .
> "Fy-ah,
> Fy-ah, Lawd,
> Fy-ah gonna burn my soul!"[28]

Fire!! embodied the spirit of this younger generation of New Negroes, aiming to cut through convention and reinvigorate a stagnant tradition. The violent terms of the foreword—"searing," "penetrating," "warning," "poking"—are a call for a full, even radical break from the standards of the contributors' predecessors; the language of "conquest" and "melting" suggests a forceful reinvigoration. With a "cackling chuckle of contempt," Thurman and his compatriots set themselves up in opposition to those they considered slow, torpid, and sluggish—characterizations that suggest they felt the old Guard was not ready for the rigors of the modern age.

The sexual and bodily allusions in the foreword reveal a major theme throughout the magazine. The subject matter of the poems and fiction in *Fire!!* (prostitution, sex, drugs, adultery, homosexuality, bisexuality) verges on the outrageous, given the context of the time. The older generation of Harlem Renaissance notables would not touch the subjects that Nugent, Hughes, and Thurman treated. Elder critic Brawley condemned the "sordid, unpleasant, or forbidden themes" that emerged during the Harlem Renaissance: "As the hectic, the reckless, or the vulgar became attractive, so did young authors tend to seek their themes in dives or cabarets or with ladies of easy virtue."[29] "Vulgarity has been mistaken for art," he wrote, and this was the worst sort of literature.[30]

Thurman's own contribution to *Fire!!* was "Cordelia the Crude," a short story about a sixteen-year-old girl who becomes a prostitute. The

story begins explicitly: "*Physically,* if not mentally, Cordelia was a potential prostitute, meaning that although she had not yet realized the moral
import of her wanton promiscuity nor become mercenary, she had, never-
theless, become quite blasé and bountiful in the matter of bestowing sexual
favors upon persuasive and likely young men."[31] Yet the story does not
adopt a moralizing tone. Thurman's narrator merely observes Cordelia,
neither celebrating nor condemning her or her trade. Compared to other
work of the Harlem Renaissance, "Cordelia the Crude" was shocking
in its subject matter and tone. Even Jean Toomer's "Karintha," the first
sketch in his remarkable work *Cane,* did not use the word "prostitute,"
but Du Bois still objected to the story.

Fire!! published a number of other literary pieces that tested the limits of
the old-guard sensibility. Zora Neale Hurston provided "Color Struck," a
play about color prejudice among African Americans in the South, and
"Sweat," a dialect story about an emasculated husband who attempts to
drive his wife out of the house that has been bought with her earnings.
Gwendolyn Bennett's "Wedding Day" describes a romance between a
white-hating African American ex-boxer residing in Paris and a white
American prostitute; and Nugent's "Smoke, Lilies, and Jade" is a stream-
of-consciousness rendering of a bisexual man's drug-induced haze.
Hughes's poem "Elevator," narrated by a working-class man in colloquial
language, describes the monotony of physical labor. The narrator exhibits
none of the ambition of the specimens criticized by Thurman. Hughes's
poem "Railroad Avenue" is an evocative work that juxtaposes urban life
—"Lights in the fish joints, / Lights in the pool rooms"—with a momen-
tary encounter between "A boy / Lounging on the corner" and "A passing
girl / With purple powdered skin."[32]

Thurman and his peers were trying to do more than push the boundaries
of acceptable representations. They were trying to fashion a new, modern
African American aesthetic that included the colloquial language and imagism of Hughes, the dialect accounts of working-class life of Hurston, the
themes of sex, interracial romance, urban ennui, and drugs that pervade
the poetry, drama, and short stories. Locke recognized this: "There is back
of this obvious rush toward modernism also a driving push toward racial
expression."[33] Indeed, the foreword and the cover of *Fire!!* weave together
the formal concern with representational experimentation with issues relating particularly to black America. The foreword's use of fire imagery
and its concluding song lyrics are suggestive of spirituals and the violence
to which black America was subject—lynching, in particular. Although
Fire!! did not include the sorts of political articles that Locke placed in *The*

New Negro, the young bohemians were "weaving vivid, hot designs upon an ebon bordered loom"—in other words, writing their version of African American modernism with the multifaceted indigenous material of African America. This agenda accounts for the importance of the form and design of the issue, and, ultimately, its anti-middle-class aesthetic. This "art approach" was new, modern, and experimental.

The agenda was evident in the way *Fire!!* put visual material on par with the literary. Indeed, Thurman saw an equivalence between the writers and "the Negro plastic artists, especially Aaron Douglas and Richard Bruce," who were out of favor with a public who wanted middle-class, propagandistic representations. Thurman admiringly saw the problem as Douglas' "advance modernism and raw caricatures of Negro types" and Richard Bruce Nugent's "interest in decadent types and the kinks he insists on putting upon the heads of his almost classical figures."[34]

Douglas' art in *Fire!!* expands on that in *The New Negro* and in other magazines and books of the era. His "incidental art decorations" are similar to those in the anthology, alluding to African masks and using geometric shapes. But his major contributions are three drawings that depart from this style. Rather than using a black-and-white Cubist style, with its attention to hard edges and geometric shapes, Douglas employs a figurative, outline style. He depicts a waitress, a preacher, and a painter with an uninterrupted line, without shading or color differentiation (Figures 21 and 22). These images seem like contour drawings—a term Amy Kirschke applies to an image entitled *Farm Life,* which Douglas contributed to the October 1926 issue of *Opportunity.*[35] As such, they appear almost to be studies of racial types, albeit racial types of bohemian or working-class Harlem. Like Reiss's types, these figures do not have any specific or ancillary reference. Yet the bodies, facial features, and gestures are exaggerated, suggestive of the cartoons of the nineteenth century. Douglas' three figures seem to be a new class of African American types. While they neither refer to any specific individual nor reflect the socioeconomic life of Harlem— problems Thurman saw in the "specimens" he rejected—they flirt with the caricatures of the past.

The coalescence of representation concerned with racial issues and a modernism of experimental form and unconventional content is clearest in the work of Richard Bruce Nugent. His story "Smoke, Lilies and Jade"[36] consists of the musings of an artist about his conventional, hardworking, striving family, his artistic work, his friends and lovers, male and female, and his rather bohemian life. The story deals with the materials Nugent knew best: the bohemian life of Harlem, the rent parties, the late-night

Figure 21. Aaron Douglas, *Waitress*. Illustration for *Fire!!* 1926. The Alta Sawyer and Aaron Douglas Foundation.

Figure 22. Aaron Douglas,
Painter. Illustration for
Fire!! 1926. The Alta Sawyer
and Aaron Douglas
Foundation.

conversations, and the liberal attitudes toward sex and alcohol. His friends—whom he lists by name: Zora (Neale Hurston), Carl (Van Vechten), Langston (Hughes), Miguel (Covarrubias), Fania (Marinoff)—populate this meditation on love, sex, drugs, and art.

Nugent explores not only themes of sexuality, drugs, and bohemian life, but also styles of fragmentation and narrative discontinuity and disorder. He rejects conventional punctuation and uses ellipses to create a stream of consciousness. The story opens: "*He wanted to do something* . . . to write or draw . . . or something . . . but it was so comfortable just to lay there on the bed . . . his shoes off . . . and think . . . think of everything . . . short disconnected thoughts—to wonder . . . to remember . . . to think and smoke . . . why wasn't he worried that he had no money . . ."[37] Nugent's account of the bohemian life he and his peers led was shocking to the old guard. Probably most shocking for the elder generation were the dreams about beauty, which takes the form of a male lover: "thru his half closed eyes he could see Beauty . . . propped . . . cheek in hand . . . on one elbow . . . looking at him . . . // . . . Beauty's lips touched his . . . his temples throbbed . . . throbbed . . . his pulse hammered from wrist to finger tip . . . Beauty's breath came short now . . . softly staccato . . . breathe normally Alex . . . you are asleep . . . Beauty's lips touched his . . . breathe normally . . . and pressed . . . pressed hard . . . cool . . . his body trembled . . ."[38] The sexual implications of the dream are obvious. In fact, Brawley singled out this story in his essay about the Harlem Renaissance: he saw Nugent's work as the epitome of the individual's "turning away from anything that looked like good honest work in order to loaf and call himself an artist." And precisely because Nugent did not employ traditional literary forms, Brawley's ire rose even further: "The pity of it all was that the young author frequently fancied that he was creative when, as a matter of fact, he was simply imitative and coarse."[39] In fact, according to Matthew Henry, "Smoke, Lilies and Jade" was central to *Fire!!*—so much so, that Nugent incorporated the phrase "Fy-ah gonna burn my soul" into his story. Moreover, Thurman wanted *Fire!!* to be banned in Boston, which would guarantee it notoriety and success, and for this reason he included Nugent's story as well as "Cordelia the Crude."[40]

The two drawings that Nugent did for *Fire!!*—presented opposite "Cordelia the Crude" and "Wedding Day"—portray figures of indeterminate sex. Each depicts a seemingly nude figure surrounded by a black-and-white design, as in the work of the late-nineteenth-century English illustrator Aubrey Beardsley. In one drawing, the figure is probably female, leaning against a palm tree in a suggestive manner (Figure 23). In the other, there are no indications of place or context. In both pieces, an abstract design

Figure 23. Richard Bruce Nugent, Illustration for *Fire!!* 1926.

occupies the left side, calling attention to the connection between design and representation. Stylized, the two prints make use of a black-and-white color scheme, but do not employ a hard line or geometric shapes, as did Douglas in *The New Negro* images. Nugent's style and subject matter had few fans among the elder New Negroes. Locke did not approve of the "decadence" in *Fire!!*—the "hectic imitation" in the "naughty nineties" style.[41] And Brawley found the themes too sordid and shocking for his taste.

The literary and visual works in *Fire!!* are clearly at odds with the answers Du Bois was hoping for in his symposium and with much of the work Locke showcased in his anthology. The themes (working-class life, sexuality, interracial romance, prostitution) and the visual and literary techniques (stream of consciousness, folk dialect, imagistic language, attention to contrast, shape, and line) are all products of a group of self-conscious writers and artists intent on constructing themselves as a new generation of modern and modernist bohemians. In fact, Locke wondered if the magazine wasn't "more characteristic as an exhibit of unifying affinities in the psychology of contemporary youth than of any differentiating traits of a new Negro literary school."[42]

While other critics condemned *Fire!!* outright, Locke gave a cautious welcome to the magazine. It heralded a shift in African American arts and letters, a move to a period in which "the young Negro evidently repudiates any special moral burden of proof along with any of the other social disabilities that public opinion saddled upon his fathers."[43] Locke was spared further ambivalence, for *Fire!!* did not survive its first printing: nearly the entire run of the magazine was destroyed in a basement fire. The magazine had cost more than one thousand dollars to produce, and sold for one dollar per copy—an equation that doomed the publication, for it could not have made that money back even if it had survived the fire. It nearly bankrupted its editors and was never revived.[44]

If *Fire!!* was Thurman's first major effort to move beyond what he saw as the problems of the Harlem Renaissance—the attention to racial rather than literary achievements, to the conventional or mediocre achievements that some thought would "form the clauses in a second emancipation proclamation"—then *Harlem* was his final attempt to construct a forum for art that explored the complex, multifaceted lives of African Americans. Thurman recognized that just as the "old propagandistic journals had served their day," the art magazines, "unsoundly financed as they were, could not last."[45] He insisted that *Harlem* had to be commercially viable.

Thurman wanted *Harlem* to be a new type of African American periodical, one that would attend to current work and be visually striking, yet appeal to a wide audience and be financially successful.[46] In a statement much less militant than Douglas' manifesto for *Fire!!* Thurman outlined his program: "It was time for someone with vision to found a wholly new type of magazine, one which would give expression to all groups, one which would take into consideration the fact that this was a new day in the history of the American Negro, that this was a new day in the history of the world and that new points of view and new approaches to old problems were necessary and inescapable."[47] The repetition of the word "new" encapsulates Thurman's intentions for *Harlem*. The magazine would be on the cutting edge; it would engage with issues of national and international importance, as well as with issues specific to the "American Negro." It would address old problems in new ways, echoing the Old/New Negro dialectic employed by Locke and other Harlem Renaissance critics. It would be "a forum in which all people's opinions may be presented intelligently and from which the Negro can gain some universal idea of what is going on in the world of thought and art."[48] Moreover, it would have a broad and popular audience, derived not from journalism focusing on racial grievances but from newly emerging literary work. *Harlem* would be the magazine for the new New Negroes and their audience:

> It wants to impress upon the literate members of the thirteen million Negroes in the United States the necessity of becoming "book conscious," the necessity of reading the newer Negro authors, the necessity of realizing that the Negro is not the only, not the worst mistreated minority group in the world, the necessity of sublimating their inferiority complex and their extreme race sensitiveness and putting the energy, which they have hitherto used in moaning and groaning, into more concrete fields of action.[49]

Again rejecting the "moaning and groaning" of his predecessors, Thurman called for new, concrete ways of reporting on African America. His was a forward-oriented vision; it demanded that readers become educated, informed, and newly confident vis-à-vis race. Moreover, he made the "literate members" of the U.S. Negro population his particular concern. They needed exposure to the new, the concrete, and the cosmopolitan in order to deal with the changes wrought by their increasing modernity.

Thurman did not insist that *Harlem* be wholly black-produced or that it be the organ for a loose cadre of his peers, self-identified in *Fire!!* as the "younger Negro artists." The magazine would solicit all sorts of articles and stories—political and fictional, national and local, written by blacks and whites—so long as the authors had skill. *Harlem* would be broad in focus. It would "promote debates on both racial and non-racial issues, giving voice to as many sides as there seem to be to the question involved" and would be a "clearing house for newer Negro literature." The "Negro reading public" would be convinced of the "necessity for a more concerted and well-balanced economic and political program."[50] But attention to African America would not be diluted. In other words, *Harlem* would be political, artistic, racial, and worldly.

Douglas' cover for *Harlem* (Figure 24) indicates that it was a magazine devoted to serious interrogation of a variety of issues and—like *Fire!!*—to experimental art and literature. The word "Harlem" dominates the cover; it appears in capital letters above a list of article titles. Below "Harlem" are the words "A Forum of Negro Life." The price, "Twenty-five Cents, per copy," appears at the bottom. Yet the cover also incorporates some images, which refer to the modern built environment and the African-inflected modernist work of Douglas. The title "Harlem" is held aloft by skyscrapers and palm fronds. By framing the list of articles with the skyscrapers (a reference to New York City) and with natural—perhaps African—images, he emphasizes both the content and the form of the magazine.

Inside the magazine appear advertisements for a host of products, services, stores, and educational institutions, especially for bookstores and publishers. These include the Harlem Bookshop, the Literary Guild of America, Tabb's Restaurant in Harlem, Albert and Charles Boni's publication of *The Adventures of an African Slaver* by Captain Canot, the second edition of *The New Negro: An Interpretation,* the Savoy Ballroom, and the Lincoln Secretarial School. Contrary to Thurman's hopes for his readers, the advertisements suggest that the audience for the magazine was local, consisting of people who were able to patronize Harlem's shops and attend its vocational schools.

Douglas and Nugent provided illustrations for *Harlem.* These images referred to specific stories and therefore seem subordinate to the articles in the magazine. There is little attention to design, typography, and other visual aspects. Thus, although Thurman seems to be embracing some elements of visual design of *Fire!!* (especially in the cover), he follows a journalistic agenda similar to that of the *Crisis* and other such magazines. Word and image are by no means equivalent in *Harlem.* Instead, the magazine privileges the literary and journalistic over the material (typography, layout, and design).

The content of *Harlem* is not as apolitical as one might expect, given Thurman's aversion to the affiliation of political organizations with magazines and to "theories of racial advancement." The first article—"For Whom Shall the Negro Vote?" by Walter White—addresses the November 1928 presidential contest between Herbert Hoover and Alfred E. Smith. The article takes the Negro as voter very seriously, assessing what each presidential candidate can offer. White discusses the choices for candidates and argues that African Americans should be involved in national politics.

Figure 24. Cover of *Harlem*, 1928.

This is not the introspective, insular stance of *Fire!!* White's article claims a place for the black population in the debates of the American polity.

Yet many of the same themes published in *Fire!!* emerge in *Harlem,* as is evident from the second piece: Hughes's story "Luani of the Jungle," which concerns a Western, presumably white man. Obsessed with an African woman, he leaves Paris, where they first meet, to live with her in West Africa. The content of the story is salacious, compared to the political focus of the previous article. The woman keeps multiple lovers while being married to the Western man. Today we see the tone of the piece as problematic. Hughes seems to be buying into the exoticism of the African woman and makes it clear that she dominates the Western man with her sexual power.

A number of other stories or articles address themes more similar to those of *Fire!!* Roy de Coverly's short story "Holes" is a description of an artist and his model, whom he discovers in a gin mill. The narrator goes there to "look upon ugly things, and to hear ugly sounds." He describes the model's eyes imagistically, as "bottomless, black holes." God "had filled those holes with the ink with which He draws the storm-clouds on the canvas of the skies, and, pleased with His work, had dropped in two moons, one in each."[51] In "What Price Glory in Uncle Tom's Cabin?" Nugent, through an account of his watching and reacting to a play, offered a meditation on codes of speech and acts imposed by African Americans. The play itself he found problematic: "No views except timeworn and familiar prejudices, and I wanted new views, or at least new angles on old prejudices." At intermission, when he used words like "Nigger" and "Cracker" in critical discussions with white friends, he was subject to the glares of "three gentlemen of color. Indeed, extreme color." Eventually they expressed even stronger disapproval of his racial stance: he was "booed and put to shame." Nugent's article was a rejection of the limits of the African American middle class.[52]

Within the eclectic tone of the magazine, Thurman couched an aesthetic position that rejected what he saw as the constricting demands of his elders. In his review essay of Rudolph Fisher, Nella Larsen, and Captain Canot, entitled "High, Low, Past and Present," he objected to Du Bois's reaction to some of the fiction. It stemmed, Thurman wrote, from his embrace of propaganda. Yet Thurman was conciliatory—he paid the senior intellectual his due: "He is one of the outstanding Negroes of this or any other generation. He has served his race well; so well, in fact, that the artist in him has been stifled in order that the propagandist may thrive. No one will object to this being called a noble and necessary sacrifice, but the days for such sacrifices are gone. The time has come when the Negro artist can be his true self and pander to the stupidities of no one, either white or black."[53]

The "Harlem Directory" that opens the advertising section of the magazine refers to the salacious, bohemian aspects of Harlem in the 1920s. It is a guide which identifies the "four main attractions in Harlem: the churches, the gin mills, the restaurants, and the nightclubs."[54] Although it lists specific churches, restaurants, and nightclubs, the "gin mills" are the most provocative: "Gin mills are establishments which have bars, family entrances, and other pre-Volstead luxuries. For reasons best known to ourselves and the owners of these places, we will not give the addresses and even were these reasons not personal, there are far too many gin mills to list here. As a clue to those of our readers who might be interested we will tell them to notice what stands on every corner on 7th, Lenox, and 8th avenues."[55] Thurman wasn't cleaning up his act. Although the magazine did not echo *Fire!!* in appearance, much of the content maintained an interest in the seedier side of Harlem.

Images play an important role in *Harlem,* although for the most part they are subordinate to the stories they illustrate. In a drawing by Douglas which accompanies Hughes's story, two lovers are silhouetted against the full moon outside an African village. This is the scene of the betrayal of the Western man. The scene is remarkable because it thematizes the hold of Africa's exoticism on the African American imagination. The technique of the drawing resembles that of a contemporary art movement known as Orphism, which employed concentric circles to represent light.[56] By emphasizing the silhouette and the African landscape in the context of *Harlem,* Thurman's global interest and desire for avant-garde representation are reinforced.

One of the most fascinating images in the magazine is Leon Noyes's *Deep Harlem: A Study in Sepia* (Figure 25), published opposite the "Harlem Directory." *Deep Harlem* depicts a police officer giving a ticket to a taxi driver, beneath a signpost that marks the intersection of 135th Street and Lenox Avenue in Harlem, one of the corners on which people advertised gin mills. Noyes employs a cartoon style, and the figures appear to be in blackface. As a printed magazine would demand, the color scheme is black-and-white, like the work of Douglas and Nugent. Yet it has more in common with racist cartoons of the late nineteenth century—those published, for example, in Currier and Ives's *Darktown* series—than with the style of the other artists featured in *Harlem.*

The drawing at first glance seems to engage in a troubling typology: the

Figure 25. Leon Noyes, *A Study in Sepia*. Illustration for *Harlem*, 1928.

figures appear stereotypical because of the blackface. But what is striking is that this is blackface in a wholly African American context. A portrayal of African Americans as the agent of the law in the middle of Harlem, the cartoon is not directed toward a hostile white audience. Instead, it is a visual representation of a literary image that was common in Harlem Renaissance writing. In "City of Refuge," Rudolph Fisher used the image of an African American police officer in Harlem to comment on the difference between the South and the North and the disorientation experienced by the Southern migrant to Harlem:

> Casting about for direction, the tall newcomer's glance caught inevitably on the most conspicuous thing in sight, a magnificent figure in blue that stood in

the middle of the crossing and blew a whistle and waved great white-gloved hands. The Southern Negro's eyes opened wide; his mouth opened wider. If the inside of New York had mystified him, the outside was amazing him. For there stood a handsome, brass-buttoned giant directing the heaviest traffic Gillis had ever seen; halting unnumbered tons of automobiles and trucks and wagons and pushcarts and street-cars; holding them at bay with one hand while he swept similar tons peremptorily on with the other; ruling the wide crossing with supreme self-assurance; and he, too, was a Negro![57]

Fisher's language attests to the visual magnificence of the modern Harlem scene and the policeman who dominates it. Like Fisher's story, Noyes's cartoon emphasizes the authority of the police officer in a wholly black context. The cartoon, however, calls more attention to the exchange between the taxi driver and man who tickets him: there is no sense of a differential status based on race—we see only one based on occupation. Noyes drew both figures in the same style, suggesting that they are on an equal footing formally. Thus, through its content and its form, the cartoon reclaims the problematic blackface cartoon tradition of the past. Peter Szondi's statement on the dynamic of change in representation bears repeating: "Prior to the collapse of the old style, the new can be discovered lodged in its interior as an antithetical principle."[58] Certainly, the form of this cartoon bears that out. Nonetheless, the context of the magazine does not suggest that the "new" has fully taken hold.

Locke published "Art or Propaganda?" in *Harlem*. The inclusion itself is significant, for it bespeaks something of a reconciliation, an invitation to the elders whose stance Thurman rejected. In the article, Locke asks a question that, according to him, had been pressing on Harlem's artists, writers, and critics: "Art or Propaganda. Which? Is this more the generation of the prophet or that of the poet; shall our intellectual and cultural leadership preach and exhort or sing?" Locke objected to propaganda, because of its "monotony" and because it promoted the feeling of "group inferiority." Addressed to the majority, it begs, pleads, argues, and nags. Art, instead, should be expressive of the group: "In our spiritual growth, genius and talent must more and more choose the role of group expression, or even at times the role of free individualistic expression,—in a word, must choose art and put aside propaganda." Locke is advocating not "art for art's sake" but rather a "deep realization of the fundamental purpose of art and of its function as a tap root of vigorous, flourishing living." Believing that the purpose of art was to afford access to the humanity of African Americans, he worried that the younger generation was not sufficiently rooted in the entirety of the African American community: "Not all of our younger writers are deep enough in the sub-soil of their native materials—too many are pot-plants seeking a forced growth according to the exotic tastes of a pampered and decadent public. It is the art of the people that needs to be cultivated, not the art of the coteries."[59] Locke was referring obliquely to *Fire!!* The "Wilde" and "Beardsley" type of "decadence" in which the *Fire!!* group engaged was not sufficient, for it and the control of the "coterie" were newer versions of limitation.

Locke's oblique chastisement came after *Fire!!* had clearly expired; it was expressed in the sort of magazine that was more cautious about things which *Fire!!* had wholeheartedly embraced. *Harlem* was an eclectic magazine that strove to expand the possibilities of racial representation, reaching backward to the images of the past and forward to the modern. Ultimately, this formula proved no more successful than that of *Fire!!*—for *Harlem* likewise lasted only a single issue.

chapter four

Them Big Old Lies

IN 1927, Zora Neale Hurston set off from New York on a two-year journey through the South. Anthropologist Franz Boas encouraged the trip, and wealthy Park Avenue matron Charlotte Osgood Mason provided the funds. "Papa Franz" had been one of Hurston's professors at Barnard College, and, according to the writer, considered her one of his "daughters," albeit a "misstep."[1] "Godmother" Mason was the patron of a number of Harlem Renaissance writers and artists. Convinced of the spiritual and mystical qualities of Native American and African American cultures, she financially supported Hurston, Langston Hughes, and others so long as they explored folk culture and spirituality in their work.

Driving around the South in her Chevrolet coupe, which she called "Sassy Susie," Hurston collected folktales from the black communities she visited. After her trip, from March 1930 to September 1932, she worked on a manuscript which was based on the material she had collected and which Lippincott published in 1935.[2] Entitled *Mules and Men,* the collection of tales included ten illustrations by Mexican caricaturist and anthropologist Miguel Covarrubias, who was also one of Mason's "godchildren," as she called them.[3]

Not only did Hurston gather an enormous amount of material, but, in the book, she also speculates about the nature of collecting folklore and the limits of the anthropological project as a viable form of interracial communication. Covarrubias' images do the "work" of illustration, illuminating and extending Hurston's complex explorations in the field of race and representation by depicting both the anthropologist engaged in her work and by evoking (though not necessarily directly communicating) the material she gathered. Hurston and Covarrubias both construct an aesthetic of "lying" that suggests the unreliability of a purely anthropological approach to African American folk culture and employ multiple literary and visual viewpoints to portray that culture. Word and image in the book thus test one form of entering black folk culture—anthropology—while providing manifold lenses on the complexity of rituals, mores, and folklore.

There is some confusion about the facts of Hurston's biography, caused, in no small part, by her notorious and calculated cageyness. Hurston was born in 1901 (or in 1891) in America's first all-black incorporated township, Eatonville, Florida. Sometime after her mother died, when she was nine, twelve, or perhaps fourteen, Hurston left Florida, to work first as a maid for a traveling theater troupe and then as a domestic for a white woman in Baltimore.[4] She graduated from high school in 1918 and went on to study at Howard University, under Alain Locke; by 1925, she had arrived in New York City. Harlem itself formed part of her schooling, as she mingled with her fellow "niggerati" of the Harlem Renaissance, publishing work in the magazines of that era. Barnard was the other important site of her education. While she was there, Boas, whom Hurston described as "the greatest anthropologist alive," arranged for her to collect folklore in the South.[5] She returned "home" armed with the techniques and theory garnered at the university.

Hurston's trip to Florida in February 1927 was the first one she would make. Funded for six months by Carter G. Woodson, who had founded the Association for the Study of Negro Life and History, Hurston had some initial difficulties and was unable to produce the kind of material Boas wanted. He demanded that she pay attention to "the form of diction, movements, and so on," rather than to the content of the stories.[6] Hurston, however, had had little training in fieldwork, having spent only a summer working with Boas.[7] Her results reflected her inexperience in and boredom with following the conventions of academic anthropology—a kind of "reportorial precision required of the scientific folklorist," as Robert Hemenway puts it.[8]

Hurston returned to New York when her funding ran out. There, she made the acquaintance of Mason, who was an "amateur anthropologist" herself.[9] The elderly woman, who felt a strong kinship with Hurston, agreed to fund a new trip to the South. Hurston would act "as an independent agent" to "collect all information possible, both written and oral, concerning the music, poetry, folk-lore, literature, hoodoo, conjure, manifestations of art and kindred subjects relating to and existing among the North American Negroes."[10] Mason would own the material, and Hurston would not be able to publish the work until the collecting was finished. Mason in fact retained control of the material (published in *Mules and Men*) until she stopped supporting Hurston in 1932.

With $200 a month from Mason, Hurston returned to Eatonville, where she set about gathering "them big old lies," the "old stories and tales" told on the porches by Eatonville's men and women.[11] Hurston identified a number of reasons for Florida's appeal in the introduction to *Mules and Men*—reasons that related to both her interest in using anthropology to get at the richness of African American folk culture and her personal identification with the region. Florida had a "cross section of the Negro South in the one state," she wrote, and the people of the towns Hurston visited had "the habit . . . [of] gather[ing] on the store porch of evenings and swap[ping] stories." Yet it was Eatonville in particular that lured Hurston, for she professed a familial kinship with the place: "I didn't go back there so that the home folks could make admiration over me because I had been up North to college and come back with a diploma and a Chevrolet. . . . I was just Lucy Hurston's daughter, Zora."[12]

That Hurston declares she was drawn to Florida for both academic and personal reasons has important implications for the choices she made in writing *Mules and Men*. The text describes her efforts to integrate into Southern rural communities in order to collect folklore, following her extended sojourn in the North. She tried to fit into the communities she was studying by participating in the social rituals of each town, by befriending its inhabitants, and even by manipulating elements of her own biography, despite the fact that her education and socioeconomic status—the diploma and the Chevrolet—marked her as different from the subjects of her study.

Hurston attempted a parallel method of integration in her writing; in placing herself within the folk culture, she was trying to write from within —as if a part of—that culture. At times, she speaks—or writes as though she were speaking—in the voices of her subjects; she employs the dialect of the rural folk as part of her own narration, in effect trying to erase, on a textual level, the difference between herself and the people in the Southern communities she visited. At other times, however, Hurston maintains a distance both in her activities as an ethnographer and in her writing. Throughout *Mules and Men*, Hurston asserts that she is doing anthropological work in order to characterize Southern black communities. By employing quotation marks and embedded citations, she claims to be quoting verbatim—and hence from a distance—the exchange of folktales, which she and her subjects call "lying." This is realism in its most literal sense: the text pretends to be a direct record of speech. This movement back and forth reflects Hurston's exploration in ways of depicting the vibrant folk culture of Southern African Americans. Would anthropology, with its aspirations to scientific precision, or the fluid and engaging personal narrative of a native serve her efforts to depict that culture? Could the written word or images (a question that the presence of illustrations in the text raises) do justice to the language, cadences, and rhythms of folktales and the rituals of African American folk culture? Or would some combination of these media be necessary to account for the complexity of the rituals, folklore, and life in which Hurston was interested?

Hurston employs an aesthetic of lying to wrestle with these questions. She explicitly frames her work as a collection of "lies," meaning, on one level, the folktales and stories that were told on the front porches, around the campfires, and in other informal social settings in the rural South, seemingly gathered according to her mentor's demands of "pure objectivity." Although Hurston conceives of her research as "formalized curiosity, . . . poking and prying with a purpose,"[13] her position in *Mules and Men* is anything but disinterested and objective. She actively participated in the various environments she encountered in the South. She describes how she sat on the porches exchanging folktales, how she found herself in the middle of a violent conflict between two women, and how she became a hoodoo priestess. In short, she became, or seemed to become, a member of the communities she visited. And she suggests that she is part of those communities on a textual level by subtly alluding to her own "lying." She creates the impression that, within the narrative, she too is inventing "stories and tales" about the communities she visited. Ultimately, *Mules and Men* questions, but does not completely reject, the adequacy of anthropology, the implied sincerity of the anthropologist, and the capability of the ethnographic techniques to record the folk forms of the African American population.

In many respects, Hurston's text is an extraordinarily valuable record of the oral traditions and rituals of rural Southern towns and of New Orleans. The first section of *Mules and Men* contains a variety of tales collected during Hurston's travels in the South, including stories about the Bible, Christianity, the origins of race, animals, magic, slavery, and relations between men and women. The cast of characters includes Brer Rabbit, Brer Gator, Brer Dog, and other animals that jockey for position among themselves. Human figures—including John the slave, who consistently outwits Ole Massa, and various husbands and wives—also populate the text. The second section describes Hurston's initiation into hoodoo in New Orleans. She describes the rituals of hoodoo, the problems that led people to hoodoo doctors, and the spells that were cast, even including "Formulae of Hoodoo Doctors" in an appendix.[14]

Many contemporary reviews of Hurston's text lauded it for its folk material and for the talents of Hurston, especially as a collector and recorder of folktales. In the *New Republic,* Henry Lee Moon wrote: Hurston "records things as they were told to her, in an intimate and good style.[15] Alain Locke declared: "Just such detached and intimate recording is done in Miss Hurston's folk-lore collection, *Mules and Men,* which has the effect of novel vignettes because of her great power of evoking atmosphere and character."[16] H. I. Brock, writing in the *New York Times Book Review,* said: "Those of us who have known the Southern Negro from our youth find him here speaking the language of his tribe as familiarly as if it came straight out of his own mouth and not translated into type and transmitted through the eye to the ear. This is to say that a very tricky dialect has been rendered with rare simplicity and fidelity into symbols so little adequate to convey its true value that the achievement is remarkable."[17] The reviewers point to the seeming success that Hurston had in transcribing what she had heard, in translating an oral tradition into the "symbols" of writing, hitherto thought inadequate. Just as William Stanley Braithwaite claimed that Joel Chandler Harris was a "providentially provided amanuensis for preserving the folktales and legends," critics celebrated what they imagined as the accuracy of Hurston's work.[18]

Hurston's mentor Boas likewise claimed that his student's text was authoritative, and in fact lent credibility to *Mules and Men* by providing a foreword. While this foreword serves to authenticate Hurston's text, much as the prefaces of white authors did for slave narratives (Boas's name and scholarly credentials—"Franz Boas, Ph.D., LL.D."—give the text a stamp of approval from the preeminent scholar in anthropology at that time), his remarks assert that Hurston has a racial authority that allows her to perform effective ethnography. He declares that Hurston's status as a black observer allowed her to gain access to what a white observer could not: "It is the great merit of Miss Hurston's work that she entered into the homely life of the southern Negro as one of them and was fully accepted as such by the companions of her childhood. Thus she has been able to penetrate through that affected demeanor by which the Negro excludes the White observer effectively from participating in his true inner life."[19] Boas raises the question of the anthropologist's ability to get into the interior lives of his or her subjects and recognizes the way in which racial difference complicates the anthropologist-subject relationship. Almost invoking W. E. B. Du Bois's metaphor of the veil, Boas asserts that Hurston surmounted the obstacles of the "affected demeanor" and was able to "penetrate" the folk culture, although her text plays with this sentiment.

Just as Boas' foreword gives *Mules and Men* an authority to describe Southern, black, rural folklore, Hurston initially claims in her introduction (which, as Barbara Johnson points out, sets up one of the frames for the remainder of the text)[20] that her anthropological training has given her the tools to know black folklore:

> When I pitched headforemost into the world I landed in the crib of negroism. From the earliest rocking of my cradle, I had known about the capers Brer Rabbit is apt to cut and what the Squinch Owl says from the house top. But it was fitting me like a tight chemise. I couldn't see from wearing it. It was only when I was off in college, away from my native surroundings, that I could see myself like somebody else and stand off and look at my garment. Then I had to have the spy-glass of Anthropology to look through at that.[21]

Hurston professes an intimate connection to black folklore; she knew the tales of Brer Rabbit and Squinch Owl from her earliest days. Yet it was only through her education, she asserts, that she developed the critical distance which enabled her to examine black folklore. The "spy-glass" is an essential metaphor here. It allows Hurston to see African American folk culture and herself from a distance. But it is this distance that would pose problems for her anthropological work. In her autobiography, she describes her first collection efforts in the South: she "went about asking, in carefully accented Barnardese, 'Pardon me, but do you know any folktales or folk-songs?'"[22] Her fancy new Chevrolet, and her "$12.74 dress from Macy's . . . among all the $1.98 mail-order dresses," marked her as different.[23] Only by saying that she was "a fugitive from justice, 'bootlegging,'" and by participating in the rituals of flirtation known as "woofing," was Hurston able to bridge the gap between herself and the rural folk in whom she was interested.

Hurston thus concurs with Boas that collecting the folklore of black America is a difficult enterprise, given the resistance of the communities to outsiders, especially to outsiders who are white. Although Hurston is racially and regionally an insider, she writes that folklore is a native custom that is particularly resistant to appropriation: "Folk-lore is not as easy to collect as it sounds. The best source is where there are the least outside influences and these people, being usually under-privileged, are the shyest.

They are the most reluctant at times to reveal that which the soul lives by. And the Negro, in spite of his open-faced laughter, his seeming acquiescence, is particularly evasive."[24] Referring, perhaps, to works like Paul Laurence Dunbar's poem "The Mask," Hurston makes a distinction between the interior lives of African Americans and the exterior views they present of themselves, exemplified by "open-faced laughter."

Hurston, however, soon shifts her tone. Rather than positioning herself as someone who exposes the hidden by retelling folklore, she begins to speak as one of those who hides, like many of her subjects. She employs the first-person plural in order to claim the status of a member of that African American community: "The Negro offers a feather-bed of resistance. That is, we let the probe enter, but it never comes out. It gets smothered under a lot of laughter and pleasantries."[25] Hurston avers that no matter how interested outsiders question, explore, or scrutinize the Negro, they will never understand him. "The Negro" (and Hurston includes herself in that "we") will be impenetrable, despite appearances to the contrary.

Hurston writes that this system of dissembling along racial lines is a response to the system of white supremacy of the United States: "The theory behind our tactics: 'The white man is always trying to know into somebody else's business. All right, I'll set something outside the door of my mind for him to play with and handle. He can read my writing, but he sho' can't read my mind. I'll put this play toy in his hand, and he will seize it and go away. Then I'll say my say and sing my song.'"[26] Almost directly opposing the claims of her reviewers, she undermines the ability of writing to communicate what is going on inside "my mind." Writing becomes a false substitute for the interior life thought to be expressed in folk culture.

Mules and Men thus raises more questions than it answers. What is the reader to believe? Is African American folk culture accessible to outsiders, to insiders, or to those who somehow straddle that boundary? Did Hurston have access to the communities in which she traveled, or was she denied entry into their culture because of her difference, or is she herself denying entry into black folk culture? Is she evasive, using writing as a "feather-bed of resistance" just as the members of the folk community use their stories, or is her work open to her readers? When, at the end of her introduction, she thanks Charlotte Osgood Mason for her financial and spiritual backing, calling her a "Great Soul" and "the world's most gallant woman," is she, in effect, setting "something outside the door of [her] mind" for her patron? Is Hurston inventing the incidents in the text in order to placate Mason and other white readers and, in fact, honoring the privacy of the communities she visited? Is *Mules and Men* a "play toy," for

Mason and other white readers? Hurston's narrative position is one of ambiguity, an ambiguity that extends throughout the text. In short, Hurston makes us wonder whether she is not, in fact, singing her own song.

Hurston's ambiguous position emerges in the main body of the text, through the events she records and in the language she employs. Consider one of the most hair-raising episodes, the fight between two women in a jook joint. Hurston had befriended Big Sweet and made an enemy of Lucy, both women who worked at the sawmill camp in Polk County. Hurston opens the description of the incident in standard English: "Just about that time Lucy hopped up in the doorway with an open knife in her hands. She saw me first thing. Maybe she had been outside peeping a long time and there I was leaning against the wall right close to Slim. One door in the place and Lucy standing in it."[27] Hurston's narration of the event suggests that she is a full participant. She speculates about where Lucy has been, as though in an aside to herself or to the reader. Hurston records Lucy's shouting with phonetic spelling and quotation marks: "'Stop dat music,' she yelled without moving. 'Don't vip another vop till Ah say so! Ah means tuh turn dis place out right now. Ah got de law in mah mouf.'"[28] Hurston immediately moves back to her standard form of narration, which nonetheless emphasizes how connected to the community she has become:

> So she started walking hippily straight at me. She knew I couldn't get out easily because she had me barred and she knew not many people will risk running into a knife blade to stop a fight. So she didn't have to run. I didn't move but I was running in my skin. I could hear the blade already crying in my flesh. I was sick and weak. But a flash from the corner about ten feet off and Lucy had something else to think about besides me. Big Sweet was flying at her with an open blade and now it was Lucy's time to make it to the door. Big Sweet kicked her somewhere about the knees and she fell. A doubled back razor thru the air very close to Big Sweet's head. Crip, the new skiter man, had hurled it. It whizzed past Big Sweet and stuck in the wall; then Joe Willard went for Crip. Jim Presley punched me violently and said, "Run you chile! Run and ride! Dis is gointer be uh nasty ditch. Lucy been feedin' Crip under ration tuh git him to help her. Run clean off di job! Some uh dese folks goin' tuh judgment and some goin' tuh jail. Come on, less run!"[29]

Hurston's position within the community is clear in the scene: she has become part of it to the point where another woman attempts to kill her over a man.[30] Not only does the community recognize her as one of its own, but Hurston, at that moment, sees herself as thoroughly a part of it. Jim Presley tells Hurston, "Come on, less run!" claiming her as a fellow with the use of a vernacular first-person plural ("let's), and Hurston indeed flees Polk County.[31]

Nonetheless, despite Hurston's status within the community, her language in this record of the event is predominantly Standard English, a formal way of distancing herself from the community of which she is supposedly a part. Moreover, by rendering Lucy's and Jim Presley's exclamations phonetically and within quotation marks, Hurston aspires to the realistic precision and accuracy of transcription. This seems to distance Hurston from the community, despite the fact that her life was threatened by the knife blade and double-backed razors whizzing through the air. This indeterminacy suggests that Hurston is both full participant and observer in this scene, a stance that complicates any simple readings of the text.[32]

Perhaps the most explicit portrayal of Hurston's aesthetic of lying in *Mules and Men* is the following brief exchange. Early in the text, Hurston describes how she encouraged her subjects to relate their tales:

> "Well, stop blowin' it and let de lyin' go on," said Charlie Jones. "Zora's gittin' restless. She think she ain't gointer hear no more."
> "Oh, no Ah ain't," I lied. After a short spell of quiet, good humor was restored to the porch.[33]

The simultaneous difference and kinship between Hurston and her subjects are clear. She can speak as "Ah" and as "I"—in other words, in both dialect and standard English, both as quoted subject and as narrator. Moreover, if she "lied" to her subjects so as to allow the "lyin' go on," the question whether she is "lyin'" to her readers, or at least to Mason, arises. Hurston's slipping in and out of the community, in and out of her actual life history, and in and out of dialect within the text renders her anthropological project unstable for the reader expecting what Boas promised: accuracy, objectivity, and truth.

Covarrubias' illustrations are a visual commentary both on Hurston's slippery stance and on the material she collected. Like Hurston, Covarrubias was a Harlem resident and an anthropologist. Born in 1904 and raised in Mexico City,[34] he arrived in New York in 1923, when he made the acquaintance of Carl Van Vechten. Through him, Covarrubias became involved with the writers and artists of the Harlem Renaissance, both personally and professionally. He illustrated *The Weary Blues* for Langston Hughes, who declared that Covarrubias was "the only artist I know whose Negro things have a 'Blues touch about them.'"[35] He became friendly with Winold Reiss, who, in 1924, painted his fiancée, Rosa Roland, with a hair comb and fan.[36] Mason became Covarrubias' patron during the late 1920s. She saw him as the "embodiment of flaming truth, moving forward on the Earth, with such a broad sweep, that all evil vibrations fall asleep on their wings of Bad impulses." Imagining that he was connected to some cosmic truth and goodness, she wrote to him that she hoped the "light of your creative impulse forms some fresh expression of your spirit on either canvas or paper day by day."[37]

Covarrubias published a large number of images in *Vanity Fair*, ranging from celebrity caricature to urban types. The celebrities included Emily Post, Eugene O'Neill, and Mary Pickford.[38] His types, on the other hand, were unknown figures who stood for common New York experiences. Covarrubias depicted not only what he conceived of as racial types— "the Dark Denizens of Harlem's Haunts," "New York's Brown Strutters, Colourful and Coloured," "New York's Negro Types Observed by Our Artist"—but also imaginary types, such as New York restaurant goers, Coney Island visitors, and pet owners.[39]

In 1927, the same year Hurston set out on her first trip through the South, Covarrubias published *Negro Drawings,* which drew on his observations of Harlem and its residents. The book contained a number of images the artist termed "type sketches" of African Americans of the jazz age, including *Seventh Avenue Type* and *Lenox Avenue Type*.[40] Others— *Flapper, Workman, Blues Singer, Jazz Baby, Chorus Girl*—are described generically and (unlike the celebrity caricatures) contain no details that would enable the viewer to identify them as actual individuals. Some of his figures, such as *Sanctified,* are contour drawings, which render the figure with a black line on white paper. These seem to be studies of movement and stance. Other drawings employ a gray scale rather than strong black-and-white contrast to create form and shape. The images, apparently studies, are suggestive of the cast of characters thought be common in Harlem in the 1920s.[41]

Negro Drawings also contains a number of pieces that depict African American dances: *Charleston, Cake Walk, The Scronch, The Stomp*. The drawings depict a single figure or pair of figures whose limbs are in physically contorted positions and shapes, with legs bent backward and hands and feet grotesquely enlarged. A number of the faces of the dancing figures seem to draw on racial stereotypes. In *The Scronch,* a dance that Hurston mentions in her description of the jook in *Dust Tracks on a Road,* a male figure wears a huge white smile that contrasts starkly with his uniformly black face. Although exaggeration of physical form and behavior is one of the hallmarks of caricature, these images seem to be also about dance and movement as racial behaviors. Countee Cullen, for example, wrote: "This young Mexican has an uncanny feeling for the comical essence behind those characters that he chooses to portray; he does not choose to portrayal all, however, apparently finding his most interesting types in the cabarets. He is especially successful in capturing the illusion of motion."[42]

Critics of the time celebrated the images for being free of caricature, despite some obvious references to ideas of black rhythm. Covarrubias himself declared, "I don't consider my drawings caricatures. Most of them are studies. They are—well—they are drawings. A caricature is the exaggerated character of an individual drawn with satirical purpose. These drawings are done from a more serious point of view."[43] One reviewer saw a remarkable level of authenticity in Covarrubias' images: "At first glance, of course, they suggest caricature. But when I looked up from my table in a restaurant the other day and saw before me a negro waiter that might have come straight from the brush of Covarrubias, I realized suddenly how almost photographic in their realism the latter presentations are . . . photographically faithful, and yet fraught with that artistic individuality which a purely mechanical reproduction, whether by hand or by camera, never can obtain."[44] In the introduction to *Negro Drawings,* Frank Crowninshield, editor of *Vanity Fair,* described Covarrubias as the "first important artist in America . . . to bestow upon our Negro anything like the reverent attention—the sort of attention, let us say, which Gauguin bestowed upon the natives of the South Seas. It is true that E. L. Shepherd and E. W. Kemble had preceded him as illustrators of American Negro types, but a glance at their work will assure us that nothing in his drawing can properly be said to derive from theirs."[45] Crowninshield remarks accord with what Harlem Renaissance critics thought about Kemble, who, he implied, did not do African Americans justice. In linking Covarrubias to Gauguin, Crowninshield sets up an alternative artistic lineage for Covarrubias.

Crowninshield's sentiments, however, infantilize the Negro. His phrase "our Negro" suggests that he viewed the Negro as a pet or child. Critic Walter Pach saw "the note of the primitive" throughout the book.[46] Thus, Covarrubias' images are difficult to fix, for they bear the exaggeration that characterizes caricature but also suggest movement and ritual. They are attempts, albeit sometimes quite limited, to capture a sense of the cultural forms of that era.

Like Gauguin, Covarrubias made a trip to the South Pacific, though not to Tahiti; in 1930, he and his wife traveled to Bali for their honeymoon.[47] Covarrubias' interest in Bali grew over the following years, and funds provided by the Guggenheim Foundation, as well as encouragement from friends such as André Gide, and Charlotte Osgood Mason, prompted him to write book about his experiences.[48] *Island of Bali* came out in 1937 and became, almost overnight, a best-seller.[49] The form of the book is similar to that of *Mules and Men*. Like Hurston, Covarrubias describes his integration into Balinese culture. He included drawings, color plates of paintings, photographs, and an index. He used black-and-white line drawings—some with outline, some with cross-hatching, some with blocks of color—to suggest depth and shape. He printed his wife's photographs and reproductions of Balinese art to introduce his American readers to the culture of the island.

Covarrubias, then, had a number of aesthetic orientations available to him for *Mules and Men:* the celebrity caricature, the type sketch, the contour drawing, and the anthropological sketch. The images that he created for Hurston's text use these styles and follow the narrative pattern that Hurston established.

Hurston herself wanted Covarrubias to illustrate *Mules and Men*. In several letters in 1935, she pleaded with him to provide images for the text and suggested a number of subjects.[50] Following Hurston's lead, Covarrubias employed a wide range of content and form. He depicted scenes and characters from some of the folktales that Hurston recorded, as well as the writer herself engaged with members of the communities she visited. These images are integral to the text; they are placed within the tales to which they refer, or directly opposite the account they illustrate. Moreover, the illustrations use the white of the page, thereby seamlessly weaving together the images and text. Although the images follow the general contours of Hurston's narrative, they subtly shift its focus, thereby providing additional commentary on Hurston and her work.

For example, Covarrubias portrayed Brer Gator as a crying, white alligator (Figure 26) to accompany some "lie[s] on de 'gator," lies ostensibly reported verbatim in the text. The first account describes how Brer Dog cut a mouth for Brer 'Gator:

> Brer Dog done de 'gator a dirty trick 'bout his mouth. You know God made de dog and the 'gator without no mouth. So they seen everybody else had a mouth so they made it up to git theirselves a mouth like de other varmints. So they agreed to cut one 'nother's mouth, and each one said dat when de other one tole 'em to stop cuttin' they would. So Brer Dog got his mouth first. Brer 'Gator took de razor and cut. Brer Dog tole him "Stop," which he did. Den Brer Dog took de razor and begin to cut Brer 'Gator a mouth. When his mouth was as big as he wanted it, Brer 'Gator says, "Stop, Brer Dog. Dat'll do, I thank you, please." But Brer Dog kept right on cuttin' till he ruint Brer 'Gator's face. Brer 'Gator was a very handsome gent'-man befo' Brer Dog

Figure 26. Miguel Covarrubias, *Brer Gator*. Illustration for Zora Neale Hurston, *Mules and Men*, 1935. Copyright 1935 by Zora Neale Hurston; renewed © 1963 by John C. Hurston and Joel Hurston. Reprinted by permission of HarperCollins Publishers, Inc.

done him that a way, and everytime he look in de lookin' glass he cry like a baby over de disfiggerment of his face. And dat's how come de 'gator hate de dog.[51]

Another tale describes how Brer Gator came to be black. The story seems to be one of ethnogenesis:

> Well, de 'gator was a pretty white varmint with coal black eyes. He useter swim in de water, but he never did bog up in de mud lak he do now. When he come out de water he useter lay up on de clean grass so he wouldn't dirty hisself up.
>
> So one day he was layin' up on de grass in a marsh sunnin' hisself and sleepin' when Brer Rabbit come bustin' cross de marsh and run right over Brer 'Gator before he stopped. Brer 'Gator woke up and seen who it was trompin' all over him and trackin' up his pretty white hide. So he seen Brer Rabbit, so ast him, "Brer Rabbit, what you mean by runnin' all cross me and messin' up my clothes lak dis?"

Brer Rabbit answers, "Ah ain't got time to see what Ah'm runnin' over nor under. Ah got trouble behind me." The 'gator asks what this thing trouble is. By way of an explanation, Brer Rabbit lights the marsh on fire, surrounding Brer 'Gator with flames. The story concludes:

> "Brer Rabbit, whut's all dis goin' on?"
> "Dat's trouble, Brer 'Gator, dat's trouble youse in."
> De 'gator run from side to side, round and round. Way after while he broke thru an hit de water "ker ploogum!" He got all cooled off but he had done got smoked all up befo' he got to de water, and his eyes is all red from the smoke. And dat's how come a 'gator is black today—'cause de rabbit took advantage of him lak dat."[52]

Both trickster tales are descriptions of origins, perhaps even of racial origins. Covarrubias' illustration, however, takes the alligator as its subject, the victim of the trickster—perhaps modeling the reader, who may be tricked and manipulated by Hurston's words. This image thus offers an additional view on the folktale and on Hurston's work.

Covarrubias also depicts the rituals of the communities Hurston described. At one point, Hurston relates how she and others overheard but did not see "Pa Henry over in the church house sending up prayer" as they sat on the porch engaging in "de lyin'."[53] There is no description of the church scene or of the worshipers, no "instructions" (as Elaine Scarry terms the images in the verbal arts that have "mimetic content") on how to visually imagine—though we may be able to aurally imagine—the scene. Hurston does not provide the words and phrases that enable us to "mimetically see."[54] Instead, Hurston records the prayer, revealing richness of the language, the cadences of speech, and the folk imagery:

> You have been with me from the earliest rocking of my cradle up until this present moment.
> You know our hearts, our Father,
> And all de range of our deceitful minds,
> And if you find anything like sin lurking
> In and around our hearts,
> Ah ast you, My Father, and my Wonder-workin' God,
> To pluck it out
> And cast it into de sea of Fuhgitfulness
> Where it will never rise to harm us in dis world.[55]

Covarrubias' image depicts not Hurston and others listening from afar but rather those praying (Figure 27). It presents rows of men and women sitting or kneeling in front of benches as they pray. The only figure with a delineated face raises her hands high into the air, while the other figures are depicted as solidly colored profiles or facing away from the viewer. Covarrubias made an initial sketch for this drawing, which is included among his papers. The sketch is a contour drawing, which uses lines, but no shading, to study the possible bodily positions and physicality of the churchgoers.[56] The final image communicates this as well, but adds shading and color to the faces and to the setting, thereby fleshing out the scene without providing any sense of the individuality of the figures. The fact that only one figure has a face—and merely a schematic one—while the others are presented in profile or hiding their faces suggests a community (the "our" or the prayer) rather than any single character. Thus, Covarrubias' image does not evoke the orality of the prayers, but gives an-

Figure 27. Miguel Covarrubias, *People in Prayer.* Illustration for Zora Neale Hurston, *Mules and Men,* 1935. Copyright 1935 by Zora Neale Hurston; renewed © 1963 by John C. Hurston and Joel Hurston. Reprinted by permission of HarperCollins Publishers, Inc.

other viewpoint on the ritual, by exploring the physicality of the ritual of praying.

Consider another example. Hurston describes her visit to Polk County, where a "group of several hundred Negroes from all over the South was a rich field for folk-lore." Yet Hurston, with her "shiny gray Chevrolet" and expensive dresses, could not manage to integrate herself into the community. There was, she writes, a "noticeable disposition to *fend* me off"; the group was using "the ole feather-bed tactics." Hurston found herself "figuratively starving to death in the midst of plenty." After claiming to be a fugitive (hence her expensive dress and transportation), Hurston was taken in and attended a Saturday dance, which she describes: "The dancing was hilarious, to put it mildly. Babe, Lucy, Big Sweet, East Coast Mary and many other of the well-known women were there. The men swung them lustily, but nobody asked me to dance. I was just crazy to get into the dance too. I had heard my mother speak of it and praise square dancing to the skies, but it looked like I was doomed to be a wallflower and that was a new role for me."[57] Hurston's desire to dance and her anxiety about being a wallflower echo her stance throughout the text. Will Hurston integrate herself with the men and women of Polk County? Will she be asked to

Figure 28. Miguel Covarrubias, *Dancing in the Jook*. Illustration for Zora Neale Hurston, *Mules and Men*, 1935. Copyright 1935 by Zora Neale Hurston; renewed © 1963 by John C. Hurston and Joel Hurston. Reprinted by permission of HarperCollins Publishers, Inc.

dance? Will she be shut out and remain the wallflower of Polk County folk culture?

Covarrubias' illustration (Figure 28) takes a different approach, depicting a group of dancers, though not necessarily Babe, Lucy, and the other individuals that Hurston names. The figures, whose faces are featureless, are rendered in black and white. The bodies of the men are white or black; their faces and heads are consistently black. The women are predominantly white figures outlined with black, and the men's hands, done in black, show up against their bodies. Each couple presents a different pose, almost as though Covarrubias were showing variations of movement in the "hilarious" dance.

This image is more similar to the anthropological records of dance movements in the *Island of Bali* than to the caricatures in *Negro Drawings*. Many of the drawings in the 1920s collection presented figures, often with caricatured features, engaged in some kind of physical contortion. In *Island of Bali,* Covarrubias published a series of sketches of the movements of the *legong,* a type of Balinese dance.[58] The series occupies two full pages; there are eighteen poses. The figure in the poses has no facial features; she is outlined in black, with some gray shading to indicate bodily movement. Thus, the drawing in Figure 28 seems to be more about dance in general than about Hurston's attempt to ingratiate herself among the Polk County residents. It provides another view of the rituals to which Hurston refers.

The color scheme is also significant, since the black-and-white pattern that Covarrubias employs does not correspond to the black-and-white racial binary of the United States. All of the figures are African American; the environments in which Hurston traveled in the South were almost uniformly black. Covarrubias was free, then, to use both colors within a wholly African American context. This is a reworking of nineteenth century conventions of racial representation. Like C. H. Warren and F. M. Senior, who did the drawings in Mark Twain's 1894 edition of *Pudd'nhead Wilson,* Covarrubias employs black and white for his figures. Yet the Twain illustrations rely on black to denote African American identity and white to denote Caucasian identity.

The plot of *Pudd'nhead Wilson* pivots on the inability of the characters to read race "accurately." Twain describes Roxy, one of the central characters, in this way: "From Roxy's manner of speech, a stranger would have expected her to be black, but she was not. Only one-sixteenth of her was black and that sixteenth did not show. . . . Her complexion was very fair, with the rosy glow of vigorous health in the cheeks, her face was full of character and expression, her eyes were brown and liquid, and she had a heavy suit of fine soft hair which was also brown. . . . To all intents and purposes Roxy was as white as anybody." But an illustration of Roxy depicts her with a black face and black hands.[59] The description of the ambiguous racial identity of Roxy is at odds with the visual image.[60]

Covarrubias did, however, include a number of illustrations of Hurston engaged in the folklore-collecting process and of the individuals with whom she interacted. *Mules and Men* contains an image of Hurston sitting on porch steps with two men (Figure 29). The illustration appears in a chapter that presents a series of stories told by Jim Allen, Lennie Barnes, and others. One man is in silhouette, while the other is depicted via a black-and-white contrast that demarcates the planes of the face. Hurston's face is white, with features drawn in black line. Her position at the apex of the triangular composition suggests her anthropological interest; in all other aspects, she appears equivalent to the men. Covarrubias' image reflects Hurston's indeterminate stance, although the chapter foregrounds the folktales communicated within the community. Thus, Covarrubias supports Hurston's explorations, yet approaches them without regard to the direct content.

Mules and Men contains an image of Hurston alone, nude, face down

Figure 29. Miguel Covarrubias, *Zora on Porch*. Illustration for Zora Neale Hurston, *Mules and Men,* 1935. Copyright 1935 by Zora Neale Hurston; renewed © 1963 by John C. Hurston and Joel Hurston. Reprinted by permission of HarperCollins Publishers, Inc.

on a bed covered with snakeskin, as part of her initiation into hoodoo (Figure 30). Hurston's narrative does discuss the importance of her being "naked as I came into the world, . . . stretched, face downwards, my navel to the snakeskin cover."[61] But it also foregrounds the elements of the ritual, her preparations, and the people who guided her through it. Covarrubias' technique of using black and white to create palpable volume forces attention on her body. This drawing thus seems more about Hurston as a female body than it does about the hoodoo ritual in which she participated. Hurston, as the nude, becomes the subject, suggesting that she is the object of a visual anthropology, an almost lascivious gaze; she is the one being observed and perhaps studied. This image raises the questions that Hurston herself has and that she does not answer. Should the reader/viewer think of Hurston as an anthropologist or as a hoodoo initiate? Covarrubias' image provides one potential answer, but the conjunction of image and text denies this simple response.

With text and image, *Mules and Men* records a sample of Southern black folklife and presents a vivid portrait of it and of its author. Hurston's style of storytelling, however, undermines any assumptions of objectivity that may have circulated around her work, and questions the possibility of interracial understanding and communication. Hurston blurs the line between the "lies" of the folktales and the "lies" masked by realist or documentary work. She tests the limits of the anthropological project and moves toward a personal narrative of her own folk culture. Covarrubias' images do more than the "work" of illustration. While they refer to the elements of the text, they provide additional frames on the folk culture about which Hurston writes. When Hurston writes about her engagement with Polk County, the image approaches the movement of dance. When Hurston describes the rituals of hoodoo, the image focuses on her. Covarrubias' images create a visual aesthetic of lying, preventing the reader/

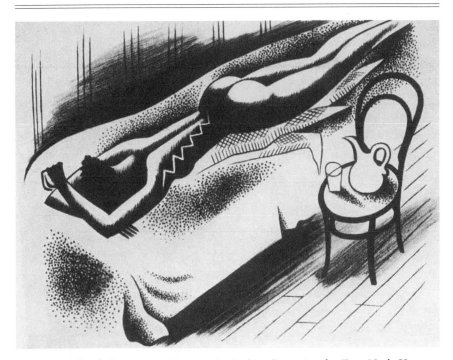

Figure 30. Miguel Covarrubias, *Zora on Snakeskin.* Illustration for Zora Neale Hurston, *Mules and Men,* 1935. Copyright 1935 by Zora Neale Hurston; renewed © 1963 by John C. Hurston and Joel Hurston. Reprinted by permission of HarperCollins Publishers, Inc.

viewer from fixing Hurston in any single role and from assuming that the "feather-bed tactics" may not be in place.

As an interartistic text, *Mules and Men* thus employs image and text to question the viability of scientific anthropology for the representation of African American folk culture. Just as Harlem Renaissance writers and artists explored ways of combating the stereotypes of the Old Negro, Hurston's work attempts to impart the dignity and creativity of folk culture, all the while questioning the ability of outsiders to understand it. Covarrubias' images support her stance, illuminating aspects of the folk culture she describes while expanding her narrative. The literary and visual together form an aesthetic of lying that seems as much a political decision as a formal one, for the dialogue between Hurston's prose and Covarrubias' images generates more questions than answers, thereby undermining the assumptions of Boas, Mason, and others, who may have imagined the power of anthropology to elucidate African American folk culture.

chapter five

Realistic Tongues

N 1937, Sterling Brown published *The Negro in American Fiction,* a survey of the "treatment of the Negro in American fiction" and of African American writers. Like Benjamin Brawley, William Stanley Braithwaite, and other Harlem Renaissance critics who imagined the New Negro by rejecting stereotypes of the Old Negro, Brown was striving to explore past stereotypes of African Americans and to connect them to the social situation out of which they emerged. The book would, he wrote, investigate "how stereotypes—that the Negro is *all* this, that, or the other—have evolved at the dictates of social policy."[1]

Brown had another aim. He wanted to document and describe the work of authors who denied those stereotypes, who "heard the Negro speak as Shakespeare heard Shylock."[2] He set high standards for these authors, celebrating "sensitive and understanding" writers who would get at "valuable truth" and do "the greatest justice to Negro life and character."[3] Zora Neale Hurston's work received measured approval. Although Brown saw *Mules and Men* as a "substantial collection of folktales by a Negro scholar," he disapproved of its failure to offer a complete portrait of Southern folklife. "The tales ring genuine, but there seem to be omissions. The picture is too pastoral, with only a bit of grumbling about hard work, or a few slave anecdotes that turn the tables on old marster. The bitterness that E. C. L. Adams recorded in *Nigger to Nigger* is not to be found in *Mules and Men.*"[4]

Brown's criticism of Hurston's work rests on his sense that Hurston avoided a central part of African American life that would help counter the stereotypes with which he was concerned—namely, the problems associated with interracial (rather than intraracial) relations. Miguel Covarrubias, Hurston's illustrator, may have agreed with Brown. The artist did a number of preliminary sketches, most of which did not result in images for the final version of *Mules and Men*. The book, primarily concerned with the vibrancy of African American folk culture, contains versions of only two of the images. A sketch of worshipers is included, with some changes, to accompany what seems to be a transcript of their prayers. A study of a man on a wagon drawn by two mules is virtually unchanged from the original sketch, though Covarrubias added a circle of dancing girls and elements of the Southern landscape: grass, a tree, and a house.

Two other sketches—a contemplative African American man and a woman bent over, apparently working—do not appear in the text, although they seem close to Hurston's interests in depicting Southern folk culture. Covarrubias did do two sketches, however, that appear to be thoroughly inappropriate in content for Hurston's text. He drew a figure wearing the white robes of the Ku Klux Klan and bearing a burning cross. He also sketched the body of a lynched man hanging from a rope, which he based on a photograph that he had collected and that showed a Kentucky lynching victim.[5]

The thematic differences between the images that appear in *Mules and Men* and those that do not reflect the text's concern with portraying the rituals and folklife of an almost thoroughly black world, in which violence, which does not seem to have serious consequences, occurs in an intraracial context.[6] Images of the overt and violent politics of black-white relations in the South—lynching victims, Klan members, and burning crosses—do not have a place in *Mules and Men*.

In 1941, Viking Press published *Twelve Million Black Voices*, which examined in word and image these very problems of interracial relations. The book contains text by Richard Wright and photographs selected by Edwin Rosskam, a photographer affiliated with the Farm Security Administration (FSA). One critic described the volume as a "sweeping picture of the Negro in America, from the first boat-load of slaves to reach Jamestown in 1619 to the present moment when the sons of Uncle Tom wend their way in unison with the white worker into the mills and factories of America. The raw unposed photographs merge into the tragic but fearless text which Wright has woven around them."[7] Another critic reported that it was "a passionate indictment of the unjust and cruel social conditions of the Negro masses, and describes their slow struggle to free themselves."[8]

These critical assessment point to Wright and Rosskam's agenda in *Twelve Million Black Voices:* this combination of historical narrative and photography would examine interracial relations in the United States and concentrate primarily on the devastating effects of white supremacy, a view—in word and image—alternative to that of Hurston's work.

The majority of reviews of Wright's work mention the importance of this combination of text and image to the publication's historical and contemporary sweep. One critic called *Twelve Million Black Voices* "a book of photographs with a running text,"[9] while Horace Cayton, sociologist and author of *Black Metropolis,* wrote of the "marvelous photographs which illustrate the text."[10] A reader declared, "The pictures are placed in such proximity to the relevant text as to be of maximum reader convenience and so as to achieve the added poignancy which skillful integration affords."[11]

As a "photographic essay" (a term employed by W. J. T. Mitchell), *Twelve Million Black Voices* exhibits "a suturing of word and image" characteristic of its form.[12] Photographs and text are mixed throughout the volume, and images often appear with captions that refer directly to the text. This interweaving of image and text raises the question of the relative value of the two media in depicting interracial relations and African American history—concerns that Hurston's text avoided. *Twelve Million Black Voices* thus foregrounds the problem of the relation between photography and language, a "principal site of the struggle for value and power in contemporary representations of reality."[13] Through its content (Wright's narrative of interracial relations from the earliest days of the slave trade to the 1940s and the photographic depictions of African Americans of the 1930s) and its form (the manner in which word and image are materially conjoined), it speculates on the possibilities and limits of word and image as ways of telling African American history. The two media are in dialogue about communicating this history, forming an interartistic book in which the text and the images at times complement and at other times are in tension with each other.

The late 1930s and early 1940s saw the publication of a large number of books that combined text with photographs from the New Deal's FSA collection. Varying in form and content, these "photo-textual documentaries" recorded Depression-era experiences, primarily of people who resided in rural areas.[14] Some books emphasized photography and used text sparingly, mostly in the form of captions, as did Walker Evans' *American Photographs* (1938). The poet Archibald MacLeish claimed that his *Land of the Free* (1938) was a collection of "photographs illustrated by a poem," rather than "a book of poems illustrated by photographs."[15] Arthur Raper and Ira Reid's *Sharecropper's All* (1941) examined disenfranchisement and violence with more text than photography. Dorothea Lange and Paul Taylor's book *An American Exodus: A Record of Human Erosion* (1939) recorded the words of Dust Bowl migrants as accompaniment for photographs, and Sherwood Anderson's idyllic vision of smalltown American life, *Home Town* (1940), contained images by a number of photographers.[16] William Stott has pointed out that many of these books tended either to expose the deficiencies of America during the Depression or to herald the progress made during the New Deal.[17] Regardless of their political orientation, these works, by virtue of their inclusion of photography and text, claimed to document reality, something that critics at the time valued.

This special claim made photography both useful and problematic for depictions of African Americans. Photographs could both authenticate the authorship of writers of slave narratives and create fictions about the happy domestic life of slaves in the nineteenth century.[18] Booker T. Washington's *A New Negro for a New Century* included photographs of high-achieving New Negroes to help make his case, and the photographs that illustrated Paul Laurence Dunbar's turn-of-the-century work lent authority to a nostalgia for slavery occasionally evident in his poetry. In the 1920s, photographs appeared primarily in magazines, rather than in anthologies, novels, or collections of poems. In the *Crisis,* for example, head shots appeared to document the achievements of Harlem's population.

In 1934, Alain Locke published his annual retrospective review of the "Literature of the Negro," in *Opportunity.* He called his article "The Saving Grace of Realism," a surprising title for the critic who had embraced the advance guard of the first generation of the Harlem Renaissance and had tolerated the left-wing modernism of the second.[19] In reflecting on the literature published the previous year, Locke lauded what he identified as realist texts for their ability to portray black America, a matter that had concerned him throughout the 1920s. Although he never defines what he means by "realism," he maintains in an earlier article that these works engaged in "documentation of the Negro subject and objective analysis of the facts" and reported "accurate folklore" that combated the stereotypes that beset the African American population.[20]

It is one thing to inveigh against the Negro stereotypes in fiction, drama, art and sociology, it was quite another to painfully reconstruct from actual life truer, livelier, more representative substitutes. But just this our contemporary realism has carefully sought and almost completely achieved,—and only realism could have done so, all the contentions of the puritanical idealists to the contrary. Social justice may be the handiwork of the sentimentalists and the idealists, but only the safe and sane poetic justice must spring from sound and understanding realism."[21]

Locke wanted "poetic justice" (though not necessarily "social justice") in his understanding, vivid, accurate, and truthful representations of black America. And he imagined that realism, rather than the modernism of the previous decade, could offer greater truth, regardless of political effect.[22]

Locke connected realism with the presence of photographs in texts. In his review of *You Have Seen Their Faces,* by photographer Margaret Bourke-White and her fiancé, writer Erskine Caldwell, he asserted that the text "pok[ed] out its realistic tongue at *Gone with the Wind* and *So Red the Rose,*" movies that nostalgically presented an idyllic South, populated by kind Southern gentlemen and ladies and contented former slaves.[23] In the retrospective reviews of the literature of 1932 and 1933, Locke counted Julia Peterkin's *Roll, Jordan, Roll* and John L. Spivak's *Georgia Nigger* among those works he admired. Both were accounts (albeit conflicting) of Southern black rural life, and both used photography to claim the very realism that Locke thought could account for "truer" portrayals of Negro life at that time. Yet *Roll, Jordan, Roll,* which contains remarkable photographs by Doris Ulmann, is a problematic account of Southern plantation life, one that traffics in notions of black primitivism and mourns the passing of rural black culture. Peterkin's text opens as follows: "Some of the charm that made the life of the old South glamorous still lingers on a few plantations that have been so cut off from the outside world by rivers, wide swamps and lack of roads they are still undisturbed by the restless present."[24] It continues in this nostalgic vein, and photographs lend authority to its biased portrayal.

In many respects, *Twelve Million Black Voices* is an effort to counter a portrayal such as Peterkin's with the same visual tools that it used and in the context of the FSA photo-essay genre. *Twelve Million Black Voices* thus grew out of the presumption of photographic realism and the FSA's rising interest in urban life. In December 1940, after working on the FSA's Chicago Series, photographer Edwin Rosskam approached Wright and asked him to do a textual accompaniment for some urban FSA photographs. Rosskam, a German émigré, had published four photographic books documenting American cities in the "Face of America" series between 1939 and 1940 and had acted as a curator for a number of FSA exhibits, including "The Farm Security Administration Aids the Negro Farmer," which was a propagandistic celebration of the New Deal programs for African Americans.[25] Moreover, he had a broad vision of the uses of the FSA collection as a historical tool for future generations. At the conclusion of Anderson's *Home Town,* he wrote: "In rows of filing cabinets, they [the photographs] wait for today's planner and tomorrow's historian."[26]

Rosskam secured support from both the FSA and Viking Press, whose editors initially imagined Wright's contribution as a twenty-page accompaniment (the final version of *Twelve Million Black Voices* is 147 pages).[27] Elizabeth McCausland has described the process: "Richard Wright did his research. Then he spent several days exploring the 65,000 photographs in the FSA files in Washington. After that, he wrote the text. Edwin Rosskam took the completed text back to Washington and combed the files for photographs closely related to the ideas expressed by Wright's text. He chose between 300 and 400 photographs, which were finally boiled down to 88."[28] Wright and Rosskam communicated about the images, but Rosskam was largely responsible for the volume's photographic look—the "photo direction," as the title page states.[29]

Of all the FSA photo essays, *Twelve Million Black Voices* was the only volume to focus exclusively on African Americans and their history.[30] It departed, however, from the models of critique and celebration of the other FSA books; it neither documented contemporary black life, as though it were something that could be recorded easily and objectively, nor celebrated America despite the ills of the Depression, as though progress and change were inevitable.[31] Although it does have a forward-looking reformist agenda, Wright's text displays a Marxist historical sweep, while the photographs focus on contemporary African American life. Subtitled *A Folk History of the Negro in the United States, Twelve Million Black Voices* recounts the experiences of African Americans from the earliest days of slavery through the 1940s and offers economic, social, and existential interpretations of these experiences. The text follows the migratory pattern of African Americans, from Africa to the South, from slavery to Jim Crow, from rural, agricultural life to modern urban life, and includes reflections on the relationship between slavery and the growth of Europe and America, economic analyses of labor, accounts of folk culture, descriptions of urban life, and hopes for the future. The photographs, in contrast, are depictions of contemporary African Americans from both the South and the North, rural and, especially, urban areas.

The main body of the work opens with a short statement by Wright and two photographs chosen by Rosskam, a combination that foregrounds the collaboration and conflict between the two forms as they attempt to render African American history throughout the remainder of the book. Wright's text meditates on what it means for whites to "know" African America. He juxtaposes the knowledge assumed by non–African Americans as they "see us black folks," who have a truer, "far stranger" history. "Each day when you see us black folk upon the dusty land of the farms or upon the hard pavement of the city streets, you usually take us for granted and think that you know us, but our history is far stranger than you suspect, and we are not what we seem."[32] Despite the assumption "usually" made by whites that African Americans are intelligible and comprehensible, something remains hidden. Whites may "see" black folks, but they do not know them; they do not recognize blacks' lived experiences or the devastating psychological effects of white supremacy: "Our outward guise still carries the old familiar aspect which 300 years of oppression in America has given us, but beneath the garb of the black laborer, the black cook, and the black elevator operator lies an uneasily tied knot of pain and hope whose snarled strands converge from many points of time and space."[33] Wright avers that there are multiple layers of meaning for African American identity. The "outward guise," the "old familiar aspect," and the "garb" are inadequate indicators of identity, perceived on the visual surface. "Beneath" them is something more complex, an "uneasily tied knot of pain and hope" formed by the system of white supremacy in which African Americans live.[34] This split—between the "outward" and (by implication) the "inward"—is a key structural device for Wright's history. His use of the first-person plural and direct address to the non–African American reader in the context of this device suggests that the writer, as an African American, will expose the falseness of this "seen" knowledge by imparting a more accurate account of African American history.[35]

If Wright's prose points to a disjunction between what is seen and what is real, the two photographs that Rosskam chose to accompany this opening passage are illustrations of this conflict. One photograph is a portrait of an elderly black man (Figure 31) and the other is of an adolescent male. With another textual context or without any context at all, these photographs could be construed as images of black laborers. Yet juxtaposed with Wright's text, these photographs call attention to the misleading nature of the "outward guise," the "familiar aspect" that whites mistake for authentic black identity; here the photographs evoke the "far stranger history." This combination of image and text thus raises the question of how each medium can accommodate the complex history beneath the outward surface, a question the remainder of the text explores.

Wright's concern is this complex history of African Americans. He imagines that he stands at the "apex of the twentieth century," a vantage point from which he can look backward and forward to determine the past and

Figure 31. Jack Delano, *Sharecropper, Georgia*. Photo taken for the Farm Security Administration, 1941. Reproduction no. LC-USF34-044266-D, FSA-OWI Collection, Prints and Photographs Division, Library of Congress.

future course of African America.[36] Focusing primarily on interracial relations and class and secondarily on the intraracial, he describes the horrors of the Middle Passage, the violence of Jim Crow, and the desperation of contemporary urban life, as well as religious rituals, dancing, and social and familial structures.

At various points Wright rejects other ways of knowing African American history and models his own historical practice. Although he does not comment explicitly on documentary photography, he is not sanguine about the ability of images, especially emerging from popular culture, to be expressive of African American life. "To paint the picture of how we live on the tobacco, cane, rice, and cotton plantations is to compete with mighty artists: the movies, the radio, magazines, and even the Church. They have painted one picture: charming, idyllic, romantic; but we live another: full of the fear of the Lords of the Land, bowing and grinning when we meet white faces, toiling from sun to sun, living in unpainted wooden shacks that sit casually and insecurely upon the red clay."[37] The contrast between the "painted" picture and the vision of life in "unpainted wooden shacks" demonstrates Wright's anxiety that the "mighty artists" of popular culture—say, the producers of *Gone With the Wind,* the film to which Locke objected—cannot do justice to the lived experiences of African Americans. They ignore, and thus deny, the harsh and brutal aspects of segregation, the insincere interaction with white America, the harsh labor "from sun to sun," depicting "unpainted shacks" as picturesque instead of as symbols of oppression and poverty. Wright's text is an effort to correct these images and to metaphorically paint the unpainted, thereby giving meaning to what he saw as the real story of African America.[38]

Wright offers a model for writing history that pivots on his sense of the disjunction between misperception and the history of African Americans he will tell. He describes, for example, the development of English among Africans, stolen from many different parts of the continent: "Our secret language extended our understanding of what slavery meant and gave us freedom to speak to our brothers in captivity; we polished our new words, caressed them, gave them new shape and color, a new order and tempo, until, though they were the words of the Lords of the Land, they became *our* words, *our* language."[39] Although the "secret language" of slaves uses the words of Europeans, it is transformed, almost aesthetically (as Wright's metaphors of sculpture, painting, and music suggest), to form a native and secret African American system of communication. In *Twelve Million Black Voices,* Wright "polishes," "caresses," and transforms language to narrate and thus expose "our" history. Using a variety of expository styles, including imagined dialogues between blacks and whites, intensely lyrical descriptions, and a first-person plural narration (just as Du Bois did in *The Souls of Black Folk*), he opens up what he casts as the strange history of African Americans.

The text constructs this history in four sections and a foreword, in which Wright describes his interest not in the "talented tenth" but in "those materials of Negro life identified with the countless black millions" who experienced slavery, Jim Crow, and the Great Migration.[40] The first section, "Our Strange Birth," offers a Marxist account of the relationship between modernity and race. Wright argues that the slave system was indispensable for the development of a world economic system, the nations of the New World, and Enlightenment thought. In Wright's history, the advances of the Age of Reason, of literature, art, philosophy, and music, are founded upon "the trade in [the] bodies" of Africans.[41]

Wright begins his historical account of black America with an alternative to the founding myth of the Pilgrims, using a structural echo of the paradigm he articulated at the text's opening. "The *Mayflower*'s nameless sister ship, presumably a Dutch vessel, which stole into the harbor of Jamestown in 1619 and unloaded her human cargo of twenty of us, was but the first such ship to touch the shores of this New World, and her arrival signalized what was to be our trial for centuries to come."[42] Integral to the founding myth of America, the *Mayflower* functions as the "outward guise" of American history. The ship that transported Africans is, significantly, "nameless" and "sister." Although in Wright's understanding it is excluded from conventional American history, it is a central and essential part of the founding of the United States.[43] Wright thus offers a shadow history, with repeated references to strangeness, paradox, and peculiarity, that complicates the familiar story of America.

The second section, "Inheritors of Slavery," moves from the origins of Southern sharecropping in the years following emancipation through the first moments of the Great Migration of African Americans. Wright describes the devastating effects of sharecropping in the South and its determination of labor, social mores and behaviors, and social status:

> In general there are three classes of men above us: the Lords of the Land—operators of the plantations; the Bosses of the Building—the owners of industry; and the vast numbers of poor white workers—our immediate competitors in the daily struggle for bread. The Lords of the Land hold sway over the plantations and over us; the Bosses of the Buildings lend money and issue orders to the Lords of the Land. The Bosses of the Buildings feed upon the Lords of the Land, and the Lords of the Land feed upon the 5,000,000 landless poor whites and upon us, throwing to the poor whites the scant solace of filching from us 4,000,000 landless blacks what the poor whites themselves are cheated of in this elaborate game.[44]

This "tangled process" of interracial relations has a "long history," which he follows through the era of Jim Crow.

Although Wright pays great attention to the dynamics of interracial and class relations, he also describes the psychological effects of slavery—what lies beneath the "outward guise" of African Americans, the "new types of behavior and new patterns of psychological reaction" that created "a separate unity with common characteristics of our own."[45] He foregrounds the way in which African Americans maintain a psychological form of their secret history from whites, by allowing them to perceive not "objective truth but . . . what the white man wished to hear":

> If a white man stopped a black on a southern road and asked: "Say, there, boy! It's one o'clock, isn't it?" the black man would answer: "Yessuh."
> If the white man asked: "Say, it's not one o'clock, is it boy?" the black man would answer: "Nawsuh."
> And if the white man asked: "It's ten miles to Memphis, isn't it boy?" the black man would answer: "Yessuh."
> And if the white man asked: "It isn't ten miles to Memphis, is it, boy?" the black man would answer: "Nawsuh."[46]

Wright portrays the instability and manipulation of language in the interracial context of Southern sharecropping as a form of resistance, something that Wright's narrative exposes just as it reveals the secret history of African America.

Much of Wright's discussion in the third section, "Death on City Pavements," refers to a theme that dominated the Harlem Renaissance: the rural African American's encounter with urban life. Rather than report facts, Wright critically analyzes the difficulty blacks had in migrating from South to North. Wright uses the "kitchenette" as a description of the literal expression of housing discrimination and as a symbol of the encounter of a rural folk with the urban form of white supremacy. A kitchenette was a small room carved out of larger apartments and rented to blacks at an exorbitant rate by the "Bosses of the Buildings." Wright describes the creation of the kitchenette:

> What they do is this: they take, say, a seven-room apartment, which rents for $50 a month to whites, and cut it up into seven small apartments, of one room each; they install one small gas stove and one small sink in each room. The Bosses of the Buildings rent these kitchenettes to us at the rate of, say, $6 a week. Hence, the same apartment for which white people—who can get jobs anywhere and who receive higher wages than we—pay $50 a month is rented to us for $42 a week.[47]

Wright, however, also views the kitchenette as emblematic and symbolic of the social problems of African Americans:

The kitchenette is the author of the glad tidings that new suckers are in town, are ready to be cheated, plundered, and put in their places.

The kitchenette is our prison, our death sentence without a trial, the new form of mob violence that assaults not only the lone individual, but all of us, in its ceaseless attacks.

The kitchenette, with its filth and foul air, with its one toilet for thirty or more tenants, kills our black babies so fast that in many cities twice of many of them die as white babies.[48]

This small room thus comes to represent the endemic violence and poverty Wright perceives emerging from interracial relations.

In the final section of *Twelve Million Black Voices,* Wright looks forward to the coming of age of the African American population. Wright asserts that black America will move forward, propelled by a variety of cultural forms and implicitly by Wright's own work: "We are with the new tide. We stand at the crossroads. We watch each new procession. The hot wires carry urgent appeals. Print compels us. Voices are speaking. Men are moving! And we shall be with them."[49] Wright ends his Marxist interracial history with an invocation of the power of print, suggesting a faith in the power of his own narrative to create change.

If one of the main points of *Twelve Million Black Voices* is to forge a historical narrative that attends to interracial and class relations, then another central aim is to test how photography and text communicate this history. The photographs of *Twelve Million Black Voices* sometimes appear amid blocks of text and at other times stand in a discrete series. Regardless of the layout, photographs often refer to specific phrases and verbal descriptions, thereby claiming at times the status of direct historical evidence. For example, when Wright states, "More than one-half of us black folk in the United States are tillers of the soil, and three-fourths of us who till the soil are sharecroppers and day laborers," two photographs, one of a group of men carrying hoes and the other of a person plowing a field, are placed amid the text.[50] Wright describes the urban landscape in the third chapter: "The only district we can live in is the area just beyond the business belt, a transition area where a sooty conglomeration of factories and mills belches smoke that stains our clothes and lungs."[51] The photograph that accompanies this description is of a house set next to a road and factories, which bristle with twenty-one smokestacks. The photograph is a visual image of Wright's textual account of the deplorable housing conditions in urban areas.

Rosskam's attempt to suture the photographs directly to Wright's text is evident in the captions; more often than not, they are quotations from

Wright's text. *Twelve Million Black Voice* contains four series of photographs that occupy full pages without any text except for these captions. In one series, Rosskam appends "We plow and plant cotton" to a photograph of a man plowing a field.[52] "We chop cotton" appears with a photograph of fieldworkers hoeing (Figure 32), and "We pick cotton" features a photo of a group of African Americans picking cotton (Figure 33). Both images and captions refer to Wright's declaration, "We plow, plant, chop, and pick cotton, working always toward a dark, mercurial goal."[53] In 1939, a century after photography's invention, Paul Valéry commented that "the mere notion of photography, when we introduce it into our meditation on the genesis of historical knowledge and its true value, suggests this simple question: *Could such-and-such a fact, as it is narrated, have been photographed?*"[54] Rosskam's choice of images of literal labor suggests that photographs, in this instance, act as evidence for Wright's historical claims. The selection process seems governed by a faith in the docu-

Figure 32. Dorothea Lange, *Hoeing Cotton, Alabama*. Photo taken for the Farm Security Administration, 1936. Reproduction no. LC-USF34-009541-CFSA, FSA-OWI Collection, Prints and Photographs Division, Library of Congress.

Figure 33. Ben Shahn, *Cotton Pickers, Arkansas*. Photo taken for the Farm Security Administration, 1935. Reproduction no. LC-USF3301-006217-M2, FSA-OWI Collection, Prints and Photographs Division, Library of Congress.

mentary power of photography, characterized by critic Lawrence Levine: "While we may dismiss ideal types, we continue, sometimes in spite of ourselves, to search for ideal sources, and what could recommend themselves better than photographic records, which appear to come to us not as the figments of someone's imagination but as objective artifacts of demonstrable reality."[55] But the fact that there is no photograph linked to the phrase "dark mercurial goal" (an allusion to the system of Southern agriculture and commerce) points to the limits of the idea that photography can be unmediated historical evidence. The photographs, seemingly "objective artifacts" of elements of Wright's text, evade issues and language where such concrete and specific illustration would necessarily be impossible.

Wright himself was not immune to the appeal of the photograph as evidence. He shot one photograph for the volume.[56] Taken in Brooklyn, the photograph depicts a sign on which is printed "Just open to colored" and a description of the rooms for rent. The text's description of the housing system that ghettoized blacks in urban areas refers directly to the photograph:

"With rows of empty houses at their disposal, the Bosses of the Buildings step in with smiles of salesmanship. They purchase abandoned properties, promising to respect the wishes of their owners, and then they immediately hang up placards saying: NOW OPEN TO COLORED TENANTS. And we black folk, glad at long last to find living spaces, rush to sign leases at exorbitant rentals."[57] It is significant that Wright's photographic evidence for his argument emphasizes the printed word. Wright privileges the text over the image even when he accepts the photograph as historical evidence. Because the sign can be quoted verbatim and because it seems to represent directly the housing discrimination African Americans experienced, Wright's text implies that his image is an "ideal source" for the historical account of *Twelve Million Black Voices*.

The assumption that photography is illustrative of historical "fact," as Valéry calls it, seems false at various points in the text. Consider a representative example: Wright connects the past slave system with the present by asserting that the justifications for the slave trade continue to rationalize the racial hierarchy of the United States.

> To evade the prevailing Christian injunction that all baptized men are free, and to check our growing record of revolt, they culled from the Bible a thousand quotable verses admonishing us slaves to be true to our masters. Thereupon they felt that they had squared conscience with practice, and they extended Christian salvation to us without granting the boon of freedom. This dual attitude, compounded of a love of gold and God, was the beginning of America's paternalistic code toward her black maid, her black industrial worker, her black stevedore, her black dancer, her black waiter, her black sharecropper.[58]

The accompanying photographs for this section portray "the black maid, the black industrial worker, the black stevedore, the black dancer, the black waiter, the black sharecropper" (Figures 34–37). These photographs cannot represent literally Wright's position on the meshing of modernity and slavery or his sense of the way the historical process culminates in the paternalistic codes. Rosskam's choice of photographs—the depictions of nameless individuals—serves to emphasize only one part of Wright's text: the contemporary and the human effects of Wright's history. The working individuals represent the results of the historical process at the center of this section. These photographs, then, do not do the "work" often attributed to photographic illustration; they do not illuminate or prove aspects of Wright's historical argument. Instead, Wright's prose seems to illustrate the material; it communicates the historical background for the photographs, undermining the "naïve, superstitious view," as Mitchell writes, that the photograph promises to be "a purely objective transcript of visual reality."[59]

The combination of image and text in the kitchenette section of the third chapter also undermines the status of the photograph as documentary evidence. Each page contains two paragraphs about the kitchenette, plus one photograph.[60] The kitchenette, according to Wright's prose, connotes death, disease, violence, rape, white profit, and corruption. Four of the photographs are portraits of African Americans: a large family sitting around a table that displays nothing but an alarm clock (Figure 38), a mother and her two children looking directly at the camera (Figure 39),

Figure 34. Jack Delano, *Maid, Washington, D.C.* Photo taken for the Farm Security Administration, 1941. Reproduction no. LC-USF34-04780-D, FSA-OWI Collection, Prints and Photographs Division, Library of Congress.

Figure 35. Arthur Rothstein, *Steelworker, Pennsylvania*. Photo taken for the Farm Security Administration, 1938. Reproduction no. LC-USF34-026510-D, FSA-OWI Collection, Prints and Photographs Division, Library of Congress.

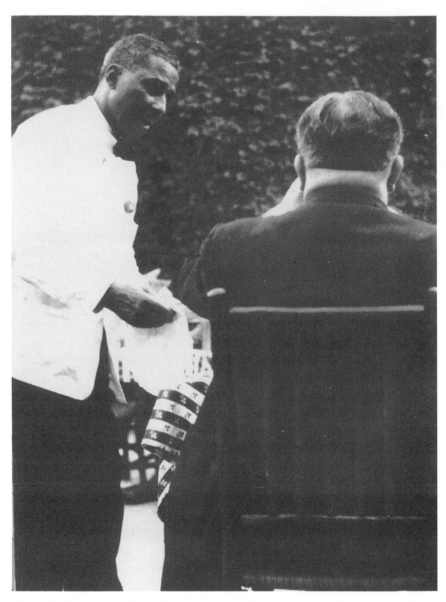

Figure 36. Jack Delano, *Waiter, Washington, D.C.* Photo taken for the Farm Security Administration, 1941. Reproduction no. LC-USF33-020988-M5, FSA-OWI Collection, Prints and Photographs Division, Library of Congress.

Figure 37. Jack Delano, *Sharecroppers, Georgia*. Photo taken for the Farm Security Administration, 1941. Reproduction no. LC-USF34-044616-D, FSA-OWI Collection, Prints and Photographs Division, Library of Congress.

Figure 38. Russell Lee, *Negro Family, Chicago*. Photo taken for the Farm Security Administration, 1941. Reproduction no. LC-USF34-038677-D, FSA-OWI Collection, Prints and Photographs Division, Library of Congress.

a mother and her children in their crowded apartment, and a man sitting amid a dirty, ill-repaired kitchen with a calendar bearing the title "Your Health" peeking out the window. Two images show the interior of a kitchenette. In the context of Wright's prose and the presumed documentary status of the photograph, these are broken-down individuals, suffering in the kitchenette and in the American racial system, which condemns them to poverty, disease, and despair. But these images are not necessarily congruent with Wright's vision; their meaning is ambiguous. The portraits in which the individuals stare directly at the camera could easily be read as indicators of dignity despite harsh reality, thereby resisting the text that

Figure 39. Russell Lee, *Mother and Children, Chicago*. Photo taken for the Farm Security Administration, 1941. Reproduction no. LC-USF34-038618-D, FSA-OWI Collection, Prints and Photographs Division, Library of Congress.

frames them. As Alan Trachtenberg has written: "The relation between images and imputed meanings is fraught with uncertainties, for, like opaque facts, images cannot be trapped readily within a simple explanation or interpretation. They have a life of their own which often resists the efforts of photographers and viewers (or readers) to hold them down as fixed meanings."[61]

Rosskam's manipulation of a photograph suggests the tension between Wright's argument and the ambiguity in some FSA photographs. Nicholas Natanson has described how a little girl's tongue, which stuck out from her mouth in a playful and perhaps too realistic manner, was airbrushed from one picture (Figure 40). Natanson reads this as erasing evidence of childhood vitality to illustrate Wright's historical claim and political orientation. This manipulation of the photograph suggests an effort to exploit the authority attributed to the photograph.[62]

Most of the photographs that appear in *Twelve Million Black Voices* were part of the FSA archive, and several had appeared in other works, often referring to themes or issues markedly different from those of Wright. The differences in these interpretations from those of Wright's volume point to the purposeful manner in which Rosskam chose to create the impression that the photographs were literal illustrations or evidence for the text. For example, in the Southern section, Wright states: "We hear that silk is becoming popular, that jute is taking the place of cotton in many lands, that factories are making clothing out of rayon, that scientists have invented a substance called nylon. All these are blows to the reign of Queen Cotton, and when she dies we do not know how many of us will die with her."[63] The illustrations that accompany this are of an abandoned plow and a grave (Figure 41). The photographs themselves and their placement in the text suggest that these are literal representations of the effects of the decline of the cotton industry. Yet the grave shot appears in James Agee and Walker Evans' *Let Us Now Praise Famous Men*, which describes the plight of white tenant farmers. Agee wrote a description of the fresh graves of "small farmers," with reference to Evans' *Sharecropper's Grave, Alabama.* "When the grave is still young, it is very sharply distinct, and of a peculiar form. The clay is raised in a long and narrow oval with a sharp ridge, the shape exactly of an inverted boat. A fairly broad board is driven at the head; a narrower one, sometime only a stob [stake], at the feet."[64] Agee's words are a description of a literal grave. The history of the photograph itself points to the indeterminacy of its meaning, but the layout and textual content of *Twelve Million Black Voices* strive to evade this indeterminacy. Wright and Rosskam's work implies that this is a photograph of an African American done in by the changes in labor.

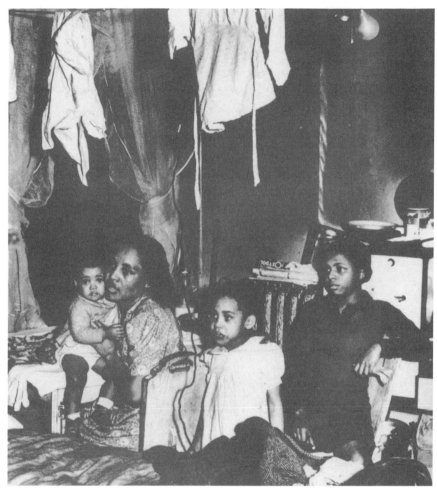

Figure 40. Russell Lee, *Interior of a Kitchenette, Chicago*. Photo taken for the Farm Security Administration, 1941. Reproduction no. LC-USZ62-31179, FSA-OWI Collection, Prints and Photographs Division, Library of Congress.

If the relation of image and text sometimes seems to fix photographs in the category of documentary, objective evidence, at other times this relation directs Wright's historical narrative. Wright begins his account of lynching early in the text, with images and metaphors. "Most of the flogging and lynchings occur at harvest time, when the fruit hangs heavy and ripe, when the leaves are red and gold, when nuts fall from trees, and the earth offers its best."[65] This passage becomes as much a vision of the colors of the land as a reference to violence, reminiscent of an earlier description

Figure 41. Walker Evans, *Sharecropper's Grave, Alabama*. Photo taken for the Farm Security Administration, 1935 or 1936. Reproduction no. LC-USF342-T01-008175-A, FSA-OWI Collection, Prints and Photographs Division, Library of Congress.

of the Southern landscape.[66] Yet the phrase "the fruit hangs heavy" is a metaphor for lynching victims and points to the interweaving of violence into the fabric of Southern society. Wright balances the metaphorical with an explicit statement:

> And we know that if we protest we will be called "bad niggers." The Lords of the Land will preach the doctrine of "white supremacy" to the poor whites who are eager to form mobs. In the midst of general hysteria they will seize one of us—it does not matter who, the innocent or guilty—and, as a token, a naked and bleeding body will be dragged through the dusty streets. The mobs will make certain that our token-death is known throughout the quarters where we black folk live. Our bodies will be swung by ropes from the limbs of trees, will be shot at and mutilated.[67]

The accompanying photograph (Figure 42), which is not from the FSA collection, stresses Wright's direct commentary on lynching. The photograph shows the bloody body of a man hanging from a tree by a rope. Eleven

Figure 42. Anonymous, *Lynching, Georgia.* International News Photos, 1930s.

Figure 43. Russell Lee, *Church Service*. Photo taken for the Farm Security Administration, ca. 1940. Reproduction no. LC-USF34-038745-D, FSA-OWI Collection, Prints and Photographs Division, Library of Congress.

white men surround him, staring at the camera. Their expressions are serious, as though they were upholding their duty as citizens. The image of the stern faces of the men and the horribly mutilated body emphasize the direct, explicit elements of Wright's text.

Horace Cayton, whose work Wright credits as an important influence, wrote of *Twelve Million Black Voices:* "The society about which Wright wrote and which Rosskam illustrated just couldn't exist in America, . . .

but it does, and for years my associates and I have tried to describe it by figures, maps and graphs. Now, Wright and Rosskam have told the story as it has never been told before."[68] Although photographs and text both complemented and conflicted with each other, Cayton was on to something, for he credits the combination of image and text with a form of truth-telling for which forms of sociological documentation—"figures, maps and graphs," the stuff of the "survey"—were inadequate.

Although image and text work together by exploiting assumptions of photography's documentary abilities, the most fruitful conjoining of the two forms occurs when *Twelve Million Black Voices* turns its attention to black religious expression (Figure 43). Wright describes the centrality of religion to African American communities by presenting what seems to be part of a sermon. The passage, which is distinguished from the remainder of the text by italics, is an example of the extraordinary lyricism—the "polished" and "caressed" words—of African American religious language:

> . . . a place eternal filled with happiness where dwell God and His many hosts of angels singing His Praises and glorifying His name and in the midst of this oneness of being there arises one whose soul is athirst to feel things for himself and break away from the holy hand of joy and he organizes revolt in Heaven and preaches rebellion and aspires to take the place of God to rule Eternity and God condemns him from Heaven and decrees that he shall be banished and this Rebel this Satan this Lucifer persuades one-third of all the many hosts of angels in Heaven to follow him and build a new Heaven . . .[69]

Wright's text imagines the voice of a preacher, while the photographs that accompany this passage depict Southern African American religious practice; they present church members as they worship. Neither image nor text by itself serves as evidence. The combination of word and image provides a fuller portrait of African America than one medium alone could ever offer.

chapter six

Silhouettes

LANGSTON HUGHES HAD A REMARKABLY long career that spanned five decades and countless poems, short stories, and plays. Born in 1902 in Joplin, Missouri, he inaugurated his career in 1921 with the publication of his first and most famous poem, "The Negro Speaks of Rivers," in the *Crisis*. After moving to New York City to study at Columbia University, he found the allure of Harlem as powerful as the appeal of higher education and, like Zora Neale Hurston, soon immersed himself in Harlem life. By 1925, he was an active and well-known participant in the Harlem Renaissance, publishing in the *Crisis, Opportunity, The New Negro,* and *Fire!!* In 1926, he received positive reviews for his first collection of poems, *The Weary Blues,* and throughout the rest of his life he published volumes of poetry, fiction, plays, translations, and autobiography.

Much of the scholarship about Hughes's work concerns the relationship between his poetry and African American music.[1] Hughes himself contributed to this discourse. In 1951, he published *Montage of a Dream Deferred,* a six-part, book-length poem on Harlem, and opened the volume with a reflection on the relation between it and African American popular music:

> In terms of current Afro-American popular music and the sources from which it has progressed—jazz, ragtime, swing, blues, boogie-woogie, and be-bop—this poem on contemporary Harlem, like be-bop, is marked by conflicting changes, sudden nuances, sharp and impudent interjections, broken rhythms,

and passages sometimes in the manner of the jam session, sometimes the popular song, punctuated by the riffs, runs, breaks, and disctortions of a community in transition.[2]

Hughes's remarks point to an essential part of his oeuvre, one that he and scholars have accentuated: its affinity to and engagement with jazz, ragtime, blues, swing, and other musical forms. Indeed, Hughes published a remarkable number of poems whose titles incorporate references to blues, song, and jazz, and he employed the structure of the blues in many others. Yet his body of work has a profound relationship to a different medium, the visual arts—a fact that scholars have all but ignored. From the first appearance of "The Negro Speaks of Rivers" to the posthumous publication of *The Panther and the Lash: Poems of Our Times* (1967), Hughes put out five volumes of poetry illustrated by visual artists.[3]

Hughes insisted that visuals accompany his poetic work. In September 1947, he wrote to his editor at Knopf, asking her to consider having the thirty-year-old artist Jacob Lawrence—whom he described as "one of the most talented younger American artists, and probably the most interesting Negro artist"—illustrate his book of poems *One-Way Ticket*. "His style would make an interesting complement to my poetry."[4] After receiving a letter from Hughes asking him to provide a number of drawings for the volume, Lawrence wrote back, asserting that he would enjoy working with the poet because his subject matter was similar to that of Hughes.[5] Although the publisher refused to pay Lawrence for the drawings, Hughes gave Lawrence $600, ensuring that *One-Way Ticket* would be published with visual accompaniment.[6] In its final form, the 1948 volume contained six black-and-white drawings.[7]

The reviews of *One-Way Ticket* were uneven. Some critics, such as Melvin Tolson, declared that Hughes's talent remained strong, while others were not so positive.[8] In his retrospective review of 1949, Alain Locke criticized Hughes for exploiting a formulaic, facile form:

> In *One-Way Ticket*, Langston Hughes seems merely to have turned out, on a now overworked formula, glibly synthetic, one-dimensional folk vignettes, reflecting varied shrewdly observed facets of the present scene. Facility, undisturbed by fresh vision and new insight, can dim and tarnish almost any talent of whatever potential magnitude. Especially with the field of seriously experimental young contenders, Mr. Hughes, should he persist in his facile superficiality, will have to surrender his erstwhile cloak and laurels.[9]

Hughes, Locke thought, had not moved ahead with the times. J. Saunders Redding, in an article in *The Saturday Review,* concurred. Redding condemned *One-Way Ticket* for being "stale, flat, and spiritless," despite Hughes's earlier reputation.[10] The problem, Redding thought, was that Hughes was employing the outdated forms of his youth for matters that exceeded them in complexity: "The old forms, the old rhythms, the old moods cannot encompass the things he sees and understands and loves and hates now."[11] Like Locke, Redding imagined that the mature poet was being "disingenuous" in using "folk idiom and folk rhythm." Both critics thought that Hughes was employing a rote poetics that relied on early success.

The two critics were correct in pointing to Hughes's return to his earlier style. *One-Way Ticket* contains poems that employ a vernacular tone reminiscent of Hughes's work from the 1920s. But the critics failed to understand that *One-Way Ticket* is not simply a volume of poetry. Lawrence's drawings are an integral aspect of the work; they compensate for what the critics imagined as the problems with Hughes's poetics. Indeed, Hughes's insistence on the presence of Lawrence's drawings implies that the poet himself felt his style would benefit from the presence of a different but closely linked medium. The central questions about the interartistic aspect of the volume become: How do the drawings affect the poems? And what do the drawings accomplish that the poems do not?

Hughes's interest in Lawrence is not surprising, for both the poet and the artist were concerned with delineating African American life and history. The poems and drawings of *One-Way Ticket* explore lynching, the Great Migration, and Harlem life. In *One-Way Ticket,* both Hughes and Lawrence responded to the African American community; the subjects of their works are African American history and African American individuals, the "similar" subject matter Lawrence referred to in his letter to Hughes. Indeed, Lawrence makes this connection clear. "I can well understand what Langston Hughes said, . . . that he would never live outside the Negro community. Because this was his life, . . . his sustenance. This sustained his motivation and spirit."[12] Unsurprisingly, the poems and the drawings deal with a number of pregnant moments in African American life. They address specific historical issues, such as lynching, migration, and riots, and important life events, such as suicide, death, and maturation.

Yet a precise account of the poems and of the drawings that bear their names reveals that affinities in subject matter cannot account for their complex relationship. In writing that the drawings would "complement" his poems (something critics recognized), Hughes articulated a model for

the interartistic work of *One-Way Ticket*.[13] The two media would complement each other, offering as full a vision as possible of their subjects.

This complementarity does not have a consistent form throughout the
volume. The poems and drawings of *One-Way Ticket* work together in a
number of ways to imagine black America. In general, the poems give
voice to but do not describe or analyze experiences of African Americans.
Lawrence's drawings, in contrast, portray the scene in which the narrative
voice speaks, representing what occurs between the poems, before the poems, or during the poems. The drawings, in other words, set the stage for
the voices of the poems, offering a backdrop for the actions, events, and
persons to which the poems refer and, in some cases, depicting the figure
that corresponds to the disembodied voice. The drawings serve as the stage
for the poems' monologues or dialogues, and sometimes picture the actors.

The sense of theater implied by the Lawrence drawings exposes a central
aspect of Hughes's poetic tongue. Hughes's poems do not speak explicitly
to subject matter he and Lawrence shared; they do not explicitly name
lynching, riots, or suicide, nor do they refer to more complicated issues of
black life (for example, the conflict between American understandings of
patriotism and African American exclusion from the body politic, which is
the theme of the poem "The Ballad of Margie Polite," or the conflict between the social situation in the South and a longing for a home, the theme
of "One-Way Ticket"). Hughes's poems circle around these issues with a
narrating, often first-person voice that employs humor, reversal, and inference. These are poems whose larger subjects are obscured by the dominant
poetic voice and thus require the reader to articulate what they do not.

Lawrence's drawings become the means by which the reader can situate
and understand the complexities of the poems they accompany, for they
depict the subjects to which Hughes's poems allude but make no attempt
to represent directly. The particular subjects—such as a lynched man, a
graduation ceremony, a funeral—are immediately apparent, for their figures dominate the drawings. Indeed, Lawrence's drawings depict the
scenes of the poems, as well as the speakers and actors. Although the figures possess undifferentiated features and are depicted in nonnaturalistic
scenes, they are the focal points of the images. The compositional technique of the drawing—the black-and-white contrast, the geometric shapes,
and the theatrical frame—are at the service of this figurative representation.

Although many reviewers were dissatisfied with Hughes's work, all
those who mentioned the accompanying visuals were appreciative of Law-

rence's drawings. The critic Gladys Graham wrote, "The splendid illustrations by Jacob Lawrence, the human relations artist, enhance and make more vivid the written words of the pen of the incomparable Langston Hughes, one of the nation's most versatile authors."[14] According to another critic, Rudolph Aggrey, Lawrence was a "rising young painter" who contributed to the "spirit of the book."[15] In fact, Lawrence had already achieved national prominence by the time he worked with Hughes.

Lawrence had been born in 1917 in Atlantic City, following the migration of his parents from Virginia and South Carolina. After a rather peripatetic existence during the 1920s, Lawrence, his mother, and his sister had settled in Harlem in 1930. He had first begun to draw in an after-school program led by the African American painter Charles Alston at the 135th Street Library. After dropping out of high school, Lawrence had joined the Civilian Conservation Corps in 1936 and the Works Progress Administration in 1938. This economic support had enabled him to concentrate on his artwork. Lawrence had achieved prominence early in his life, in 1941, with the publication in *Fortune* magazine of almost half of his most famous work: a sixty-panel sequence of paintings entitled *The Migration of the Negro*.[16]

Lawrence's major works are narrative, historical series whose subject is African American history. These include the *Migration Series,* the *Harriet Tubman Series,* and the *Frederick Douglass Series,* all of which explicitly refer to specific, political events or personages. Composed of small, numbered paintings with text by Lawrence at the bottom of each frame, they act almost as revisionary textbooks.[17] Lawrence had in fact done a great deal of historical research for the series, spending many hours in the Schomburg Collection of the 135th Street branch of the New York Public Library.[18]

Lawrence's style complements this historical aim. His compositional technique involved the use of flat shapes layered on one another as a collage; these were combined with a strong line and a narrative, sequential format. Lawrence employed primary colors and earth pigments, thereby eliminating the distractions of chiaroscuro or tone from the subject matter. The net effect of this aesthetic stance was to make the subject monumental and epic. His works suggest a single, narrative strain, uncomplicated by subtle variations of shade, light, or interpretation. And his technique implies that this single strain directed his work from its beginnings. He conceived of his series as a whole from the outset. Only after drawing the basic elements of each of the individual frames did he use color. He applied a single color to each frame that required it, establishing a uniform palette for the series. Thus, through subject matter, research, and form, Lawrence composed paintings that function as direct historical narrative.

On May 5, 1948, Lawrence wrote to Hughes declaring that he was going to illustrate the poem called "Flight."[19] The volume contains no drawing with this title. Instead, there is one entitled *Silhouette,* ostensibly referring to the poem "Silhouette," which precedes the drawing and follows "Flight."[20] After a close consideration of the poems and the drawing, it becomes clear that the visual medium depicts what occurs between the two poems, thereby providing a tableau, a theatrical backdrop, for their voices. The effect of this is to balance Hughes's poetics of indirection, distance, and understatement with a visual aesthetic of somber direction.

"Flight" begins with a direct address to a black man being pursued by a white lynch mob:

> Plant your toes in the cool swamp mud.
> Step, and leave no track.
> Hurry, sweating runner!
> The hounds are at your back.

Immediately, Hughes establishes a distance between the narrator of the poem (and hence the reader) and the man who is its subject. The imperatives "plant," "step," and "hurry" convey a sense of urgency and danger directed at the protagonist by a narrator obviously watching the chase. The man responds (in italics, a visual marker of his voice), *"No, I didn't touch her. / White folks ain't for me."* It becomes clear, then, that the cause of the subsequent lynching is an accusation of some kind of sexual contact between a black man and a white woman. The futility of the black man's assertions in the face of the accusation is painfully apparent. His "No" does not have any effect on the situation, for the narrating voice surfaces again in the poem, framing the voice of the chased man: "Hurry, black boy, hurry! / Or they'll hang you to a tree!" The poem thus concludes without resolution of the chase; the moment is suspended in a place, "the cool swamp mud," though it alludes to the horror of the outcome.[21]

This, then, is not only a poem about a possible lynching, but also a poem about the futility of finding truth within a bankrupt racial system, founded on a series of racial myths and violence. The futile "No" of the italicized second voice cannot compete with the repeated imperative or with the simply stated prophecy "They'll hang you to a tree!"

"Silhouette," the following poem, offers a slightly more vivid sense of place than "Flight." In the "dark of the moon," we see the roadside tree from which the man was hanged—a trope familiar from many other works, such as Paul Laurence Dunbar's poem "The Haunted Oak." We are also given a glimpse into the mindset of the white folks who lynch:

> They've hung a black man
> To a roadside tree
> In the dark of the moon
> For the world to see
> How Dixie protects
> Its white womanhood.

The poem clearly plays upon the position of the Southern female, referred to in the earlier poem. She is the "gentle lady" protected by the violence of the white male, a woman the poem urges not to "swoon." The contradictions of this action become clear, through the incongruity of the words "gentle" and "swoon" with the lynch mob. The final warning to the "Southern lady" takes on additional meaning, complicating any sense of innocence: "Be good / Be good" perhaps warns her not to participate in the racial system, or perhaps gives her some agency by recognizing her sexual contact with the lynched black man.[22]

"Silhouette" is immediately recognizable as a continuation of "Flight." This poem, too, employs direct address and imperative:

> Southern gentle lady,
> Do not swoon.
> They've just hung a black man
> in the dark of the moon.

The poetic voice is the same, distant from the man fleeing from lynching in the first poem and from the other potential voices. Moreover, lines are repeated from the previous poem: "They've just hung a black man / In the dark of the moon." But there is an important difference between the two poems—namely, the shift from the future tense of "Flight" ("they'll hang you") to the recent past of "Silhouette" ("They've just hung"). Where is the present tense which has "just" passed? It is in Lawrence's illustration.

The drawing *Silhouette* (Figure 44) depicts what transpires between the two poems; it follows "Flight" and directly precedes—temporally—"Silhouette." It is a visual representation of what has "just" occurred. The black-and-white drawing, reminiscent of a woodcut, presents the lynched black man, eyes open, hanging from a tree. The composition of the painting is vertical. The tree occupies the top half and the body of the man the bottom half. The rope links the two, revealing the tension, the strength of

Figure 44. Jacob Lawrence, *Silhouette*. Illustration for Langston Hughes, *One-Way Ticket*, 1949. Copyright © 2003 Gwendolyn Knight Lawrence / Artists Rights Society (ARS), New York. Courtesy of the Houghton Library, Harvard University.

the racial system, alluded to by the rope itself. The man's body hangs slack; his face is frozen in a mask-like grimace, looking down.

The presentation of this scene contrasts radically with that of the poems. The drawing depicts the body that was evoked only as the source of a panic-stricken voice in "Flight." Yet the distance that is apparent in the poem is not rendered. The viewer does not watch the Southern white woman watching the black man; she does not function as an intermediary. Instead, the viewer is in her position, looking at the lynched man, maybe even swooning at the violence, the pain in the man's face and slack limbs, or the starkness of the black-and-white contrast.

Lawrence had previously composed works that portrayed scenes of lynching or referred to lynching. For example, Panel 15 of the *Migration Series,* a horizontal image, shows a figure sitting almost in a fetal position with his or her back to the viewer, to the left of a branch from which a noose hangs. The colors of the landscape are neutral, beige and brown, while the figure is rendered in deep red. The noose, dark brown and black, stands out from the landscape. In contrast to the image in *One-Way Ticket,* this painting does not depict the body itself. And the caption, rather than describing this particular lynching, speaks of lynching more broadly, as a reason for the Great Migration: "Another cause was lynching. It was found that where there had been a lynching, the people who were reluctant to leave at first left immediately after this." This is akin to Hughes's poetics of indirection. Perhaps it was the intervention of the poems, which function much like Lawrence's captions, that prompted Lawrence to be more explicit.

That Lawrence uses black-and-white contrast in *One-Way Ticket,* as opposed to his standard primary colors, is significant. His technique here stems in part from the physical demands of the printing process: it is easier to reproduce black-and-white drawings than color paintings. Since black-and-white rendering is often used to give an impression of objectivity, one might attribute Lawrence's use of the technique to his desire to narrate history. But given his use of color in the series, this seems unlikely. Rather, the stark contrast alludes to the black-and-white relations at the heart of some of the poems. The strong, unmediated contrast between the colors articulates a strong racial conflict. The looming white areas allude to the individuals and the system that lynch the black man.

Like the *Migration Series* panel and Hughes's poems, Lawrence's *Silhouette* strips the scene of distinguishing features. The black-white contrast and the geometric shapes do not allow distractions of shadow or variations of tone. Lawrence himself wrote about these twin pulls in his work: "The human subject is the most important thing. My work is abstract in the sense of having been designed and composed, but is not abstract in the sense of having no human content. . . . [I] want to communicate. I want the idea to strike right away."[23] The abstraction and focus of the human figure in the drawing, however, do have a different effect from that of Hughes's poem, which emphasizes voice and aesthetic distance, and from that of the *Migration Series* panel, which does not visualize the act of lynching. Lawrence's drawing, through its strong black-and-white geometric contrasts and its focus on the body, seems louder, more direct, and more explicit than the poems for which it sets the stage, thereby making the "human content" refer to race relations.

The poem "The Ballad of Margie Polite," with its accompanying drawing, employs a slightly different interaction between the visual and the poetic. The poem refers to a riot that occurred on August 1, 1943, in Harlem. A black woman, Margie Polite, was having a fight with a white policeman. When a black soldier, returning from wartime duty, intervened, the policeman shot him. Mistakenly believing that the soldier had died, Polite ran into the street screaming that he had been killed. In the ensuing riot, four people died, five hundred were injured, and approximately five million dollars in damage was caused.[24]

The ballad form makes the poem read like a nursery rhyme:

> If Margie Polite
> Had of been white
> She might not've cussed
> Out the cop that night.
>
> In the lobby
> Of the Braddock Hotel
> She might not've felt
> The urge to raise hell.

The poem sounds almost like a child's history of the creation of Margie's Day. Indeed, Hughes saw a certain dark humor in the riot ("I don't know why [it] tickles me, and I am sorry in my soul"), and this humor became the poem's basic means of operation, establishing an ironic distance between the narrator and the event.[25] The poem deals not so much with the riot as with the humorous incongruities behind it. Margie Polite, who started the riot with her mistaken screaming, comes to the fore in the poem through the repetition of her name. Hughes thus calls attention to the arbitrary, accidental nature of history in which a holiday can emerge in honor of an unlikely hero:

> Mark August 1st
> As Decreed by fate
> For Margie and History
> To have a date.

Moreover, by continually referring to holidays, the poem reverses conventional expectations about which members of a community are worth honoring. It is not the soldier who becomes the hero, as one might expect, but the accidental, hysterical Margie. It is not the race leaders who are successful in communicating their message to the black masses ("Go home yo hucks, / They didn't kill the soldier"), but the addled Margie.[26]

The poem, then, assumes a post-riot place, establishing a temporal distance. It reflects on the event but does not decry its violence. Rather, the question it addresses is one that extends beyond the scope of the event itself. It examines the disenfranchisement of the black community within the United States, to such an extent that alternative holidays ("It wasn't Mother's / Nor Father's— / It were / MARGIE'S DAY!") are established. The poem represents the myth of a founding mother, one who occupies an alternative position, who becomes an alternative political leader capable of speaking the language of the black masses better than the inadequate race leader (explicitly named), and who has greater political effect: "It is Margie Polite! Margie Polite / [Who] kept the Mayor / and Walter White / And Everybody up all night."[27]

Lawrence's drawing (Figure 45) presents a very different version of the riot, calling attention to the violence and confusion of the event. Because it is meant to precede the poem temporally, the drawing alludes to its use of multiple voices. Although the narrator's voice dominates in the poem, the words of rioters intrude. Visually differentiated from the narrating voice by italics, rioters yell: *"They killed a colored soldier!"* and *"Naw! But they tried."* Lawrence represents these competing voices more violently, through the harshness and busyness of the composition. In the *Migration Series,* he had presented a number of panels that referred to riots. Yet none of the panels had depicted the sort of out-of-control violence evident in the *One-Way Ticket* drawing. Panel 50 portrays white workers attacking black strikebreakers, and Panel 51 refers to riots by depicting flames emerging from buildings. Only Panel 52 contains figures that are similar to those of *The Ballad of Margie Polite:* five figures wielding knives, sticks,

Figure 45. Jacob Lawrence, *The Ballad of Margie Polite*. Illustration for Langston Hughes, *One-Way Ticket*, 1949. Copyright © 2003 Gwendolyn Knight Lawrence / Artists Rights Society (ARS), New York. Courtesy of the Houghton Library, Harvard University.

and fists. But it is a much simpler composition and clearly does not attempt to represent the multiplicity of voices characteristic of Hughes's poems.

The competing diagonals of *The Ballad of Margie Polite* create a sense of the chaos of the riot. Lawrence's drawing presents a dialogue of shapes, but it is a dialogue predicated on violence—the shapes battle one another, whereas Hughes's voices conflict in a darkly humorous way. The immediacy of the intracommunity violence (deemphasized by the holiday focus of the poem) comes through in the framing of the drawing, which crops various body parts. An arm surfaces at the lower center; half a child exits on the left; a foot occupies the upper left corner. These quasi-dismemberments, the layerings of body on body, and the continuance of bodies outside the drawing have the effect of stressing the confusion, the unending quality of the riot, and the horror of violence within the African American community.

The anguish in the unindividuated faces, the large hands holding weapons, and the fists all give a sense of the pain caused by the action. Lawrence extends this pain to a general statement by his use of stylization, which creates the impression that the flailing bodies are an infinitely reproducible pattern. Almost like Egyptian hieroglyphs, Lawrence's graphic representations act as a kind of shorthand for representing members of the black community in conflict with white figures of authority.

Lawrence composed a drawing to accompany the poem "One-Way Ticket," and ensured that the two were tightly interconnected. Both works refer to the migration of African Americans from the South to the North and Midwest during the first half of the twentieth century. But the subject matter alone does not do justice to their relationship. The poem employs a first-person singular, and the drawing presents the voice in the form of a body staring out of the picture plane.

The narrator begins the first, second, and third stanzas of the four-stanza poem with the same words: "I pick up my life and take it"—"with me" or "on the train" or "away." The portability of a life that can be picked up is a product of the Jim Crow laws:

> People who are cruel
> and afraid
> who lynch and run,
> who are scared of me
> And me of them.

In this understated tone, the narrator matter-of-factly describes a search for a place defined only as being "not Dixie" or "not South." The speaker can see the specific places for which he aims, and names them: Chicago, Detroit, Los Angeles, Bakersfield. The South and Dixie, from which he flees, are, in contrast, general locations, a broad mindset.[28]

In his flight, the narrator points to a fundamental despair mixed with frustration: "I am fed up," he declares. The frustration, however, is not resolved by the migration itself. It appears most clearly at the end, when the cities for which the narrator aims come to be abstracted much like the South or Dixie:

> I pick up my life
> And take it away
> On a one-way ticket—
> Gone up North,
> Gone out West,
> Gone!

The frustration is clearest here: an abstract "gone," not here or there, is the final state for the narrator. There are no adjectives, no descriptions to individuate place, except for the cruel, fearful people who populate the South. The flight from Dixie toward a someplace else defined via negation is a response to the political situation.

Lawrence's drawing (Figure 46) makes the journey of the Great Migration abstract in much the way that Hughes's adjective-less poem does. First, it depicts the general event described by the poem itself: the moment of the journey. It shows a number of people, presumably in a station, dressed in traveling clothes and sitting on pieces of luggage. Are their lives in those boxes and suitcases? That seems to be the implication. Second, the drawing refers to the transitory, to the passage that is at the heart of Hughes's poem. But the poem provides a past and a future, a start and an end. The drawing locates itself in the moment of the poem, almost acting as a stage set from which the narrator—in the person of a young boy—stares out.

In the poem "One-Way Ticket," the narrator participates in the event, dismantling the aesthetic distance present in the other poems; instead, the poem maintains a sense of distance by virtue of the narrator's transitory, abstract state. In the drawing, the boy in the foreground stares out at us, almost commenting on the migrating figures that dominate the right half of the picture plane. He has distinguishing features: eyes, eyebrows, a nose, a mouth, shorts, a shirt, a hat. Compared to the majority of figures in the drawing, he is super-individuated. The other figures have at most a single eye; generally they have no facial features at all.

Figure 46. Jacob Lawrence, *One-Way Ticket*. Illustration for Langston Hughes, *One-Way Ticket*, 1949. Copyright © 2003 Gwendolyn Knight Lawrence / Artists Rights Society (ARS), New York. Courtesy of the Houghton Library, Harvard University.

The vertical movement—from the lower right to the upper left—represents the physical movement of the migration. And the black background is the analogue of Hughes's lack of adjectives and adverbs. This technique confines the figures, just as their lives are confined, bundled up, and shrunk into the moment of their journey. The fleeting and the transitory are hallmarks of the experience of the Great Migration.[29]

Both poem and drawing articulate, in a generalized way, the disruption caused by this pivotal moment in twentieth-century African American history. Through the juxtaposition of abstract location and first-person narration, the poem implies that the migration is a universal African American experience. Likewise, Lawrence's drawing moves the subject to a more general focus, using abstracted, unindividuated figures.

The first poem in which Hughes addresses a nonhistorically specific moment is "Too Blue." The poem renders the voice of a person contemplating suicide. It is not easily susceptible to visual representation, because it is concerned primarily with the narrator's state of mind. In the earlier poems, the direct references to African American history made Lawrence's task easier. His drawing *Too Blue* (Figure 47) would have posed some problems, if his aim had been merely to illustrate the poem. Fortunately, he did not attempt to reproduce Hughes's poem in visual form. Rather, *Too Blue* presents the occasion of the poem's making, the individual whose thought process we overhear. The drawing depicts a man with his back to us, sitting on a bed in an empty room with bare closet, bare light bulb, white walls relieved by a flower pattern. This is a remarkably banal and everyday scene—though a bleak one—when juxtaposed with the ostensible subject of the poem.

The poem opens with a song-like refrain:

> I got those sad old weary blues.
> I don't know where to turn.
> I don't know where to go.
> Nobody cares about you
> When you sink so low.

The third line of the second stanza is a shocking question: "Shall I take a gun and put myself away?" But it is tempered by the reversal in the following stanza: "I wonder if / One bullet would do? / As hard as my head is, / It would probably take two." The lines take the earlier question regarding method to its most absurd and humorous conclusion. This is Hughes's comic effect, the one which acknowledges the bubbling up of the desire for self-assertion ("My head is so hard") despite the feelings of loneliness

Figure 47. Jacob Lawrence, *Too Blue*. Illustration for Langston Hughes, *One-Way Ticket*, 1949. Copyright © 2003 Gwendolyn Knight Lawrence / Artists Rights Society (ARS), New York. Courtesy of the Houghton Library, Harvard University.

("Nobody cares"), almost as if the narrator were directly addressing those he implicates in the word "Nobody."[30]

The reversal at the end returns to the somber tone, emphasizing another thing the narrator lacks:

> But I ain't got
> Neither bullet nor gun—
> And I'm too blue
> To look for one.[31]

The poem ends with a move in two directions: the feeling of being too blue even to attempt suicide, which requires a certain amount of agency, and the wry self-assertion which maintains the narrator through that desire.

The contrasts in the drawing—between the flowered wallpaper and the bleak emptiness of the interior, between the solidity of the figure's back and the droop of the head—reflect the competing instincts in the poem. The room is stark and cold, yet the flowers indicate some kind of agency: an effort has been made to turn the place into a welcoming home. Likewise, the sturdy back is juxtaposed with the defeated head. The comic force of the poem is absent from the drawing, but the mechanism of contrast echoes the poet's technique. Although Lawrence's somber version of Rodin's *Thinker* does not see the redemption that Hughes's narrator does, the drawing and the poem are closely aligned.

Lawrence's drawing *Home in a Box* and Hughes's poem "Deceased" follow a similar structure. Hughes's poem is a brief account of a man's death:

> Harlem
> Sent him home
> In a long box—
> Too dead
> To know why:
>
> The licker
> Was lye.

The poem contains Hughes's typical poetics of humorous reversal. The gravity of a death is tempered by a comic turn at the end of the poem.

As in *Too Blue,* Lawrence's drawing extrapolates from this poem to envision the scene the poem invents. The drawing imagines "Harlem," the community grieving for the dead man. A long line of mourners file past a coffin, the box of the title, which lies at the foreground of the image. A

Figure 48. Jacob Lawrence, *Home in a Box*. Illustration for Langston Hughes, *One-Way Ticket*, 1949. Copyright © 2003 Gwendolyn Knight Lawrence / Artists Rights Society (ARS), New York. Courtesy of the Houghton Library, Harvard University.

body is displayed in the coffin. A solid mass of black, indicating the open space at the funeral, occupies the right side of the image.

Lawrence depicts the figures with a black-and-white geometric contrast, rendering them solid and monumental as they mourn. The jagged lines that depict their clothing refer to the pain of the scene. The humor of Hughes's poem, evident in the rhyme ("why," "lye") and the colloquial pronunciation of liquor ("licker"), is nowhere evident in the drawing. Again, Lawrence's visual depiction calls attention to a serious aspect of life—a community in grief—that Hughes alludes to only in a brief phrase: "Harlem / Sent him home." Lawrence's monumental drawing—with its mass of black on the right side and the solid figures grimacing in pain—compensates for Hughes's poetics of indirection (Figure 48).

It is difficult to point to a single interartistic aesthetic in the book *One-Way Ticket*. Still, it is clear that the poems and drawings act together to represent moments, events, or personages in African America, through common subject matter and technique. For example, Hughes focuses on narrative voice throughout the volume. Although he concentrates on the first-person singular, he includes other voices to represent the complexity of the events described. Lawrence's collage aesthetic and his layering of forms serve as visual parallels to the multiple voices.

The poems and drawings are effective together because each medium compensates for the limits of the other. While Hughes's body of poetry offers a spectrum of possibilities, ranging from humorous aphorisms to explicit, angry political commentary, *One-Way Ticket* tends to employ indirection and inference as its governing aesthetic principle. Thus, the ostensible subject matter is often complex and may be implied by the tone, by antitheses and reversals, and by the multiplicity of voices. Lawrence's drawings, in contrast, make the subject matter explicit.

Then what is the significance of the common tongue of the poems and drawings? The two media complement each other, providing different lenses on the same subject, asserting the centrality of these subjects for aesthetic representation. The distinctions and parallels between the two aesthetics make the volume more powerful. The crossing of boundaries between drawing and poetry, movement born of a desire to represent African American social issues and the complexity of black life, allows the reader a more nuanced vision.

Epilogue: Newer Negroes

> Do we confront today on the cultural front another Negro,
> either a new Negro or a maturer "New Negro"?
>
> —Alain Locke, "The Negro: 'New' or Newer" (1939)

ARLY IN 1939, Alain Locke published an annual review of the
"literature of the Negro." Entitled "The Negro: 'New' or Newer," his article compared the literary work that had emerged fifteen years—"nearly
half a generation"—before with that of the "new generation of creative
talent" of the 1930s. For Locke, the central question was whether the
youth of the past had matured or a countermovement—one that embraced
a "new ideology with a changed world outlook and social orientation"—
had emerged from African American arts and letters.[1]

Locke preferred the former idea: he believed that, after a "frothy adoles-
cence," the New Negro movement had become a mature artistic *and* social
movement.[2] He was so sure of this evolution that he was planning a new
book, tentatively titled *The New Negro: Fifteen Years Later,* or perhaps
The Newer Negro: 1939. The volume would be similar in format and content to the first anthology: it would contain essays, fiction, and poetry,
along with color and black-and-white illustrations. Rather than a section
entitled "The New Negro in a New World," which the 1925 anthology
contained, this 1939 collection would include a one entitled "The Negro in
a New South and a New Social Order."[3]

Locke planned to publish short stories and poems by Sterling Brown,
Countee Cullen, Langston Hughes, Zora Neale Hurston, Richard Wright,
and others. Aaron Douglas would provide the visual material. The work of
these new New Negroes, Locke imagined, would fulfill the "social aspect
of the New Negro front" established in the 1920s: "Today's literature and

art, an art of searching social documentation and criticism, thus becomes a consistent development and matured expression of the trends that were seen and analyzed in 1925."[4]

Despite Locke's attempt to gather the writers and artists of the late 1930s into the New Negro movement of the 1920s, he had criticism for Hurston, Wright, Hughes, and others. In his retrospective review of 1939, he wrote of Hurston: "Too much of *Tell My Horse* is anthropological gossip in spite of many unforgettable word pictures."[5] His criticism of Hughes was more direct and scathing: in *One-Way Ticket,* Hughes was turning out "a now overworked formula, glibly synthetic, one-dimensional folk vignettes."[6]

Of Wright's *Twelve Million Black Voices,* Locke wrote: "This is an important book."[7] Yet he accused Wright, who focused on the masses of African Americans rather than the talented tenth, of creating a unitary Negro: "The fallacy of the 'new' as of the 'older' thinking is that there is a type Negro who, either qualitatively or quantitatively, is the type symbol of the entire group. To break arbitrary stereotypes it is necessary perhaps to bring forward counter-stereotypes, but none are adequate substitutes for the whole truth. There is, in brief, no 'The Negro.'" What Locke wanted was a more complete account of African American life: "We must become aware of the class structure of the Negro population, and expect to see, hear and understand the intellectual elite, the black bourgeoisie as well as the black masses."[8]

Locke had kinder words for visual artists. From the Harlem Renaissance, when the "Negro artist found his place beside the poets and writers of the 'New Negro' movement," to the 1940s, artists, he claimed, were sensitive to the heterogeneity of the African American population.[9] Visual art, according to Locke in 1945, had "ripened and flowered."[10] The variety of styles—a "growing democracy in American art"—had "broken through the limiting stereotypes through which we traditionally saw Negro life and the Negro."[11] He praised Jacob Lawrence and the "intuitive genius of [this] New York lad."[12] He applauded Richmond Barthé's "original talent and steadily maturing artistic stature."[13]

This curious split between Locke's critique of the so-called mature New Negro writers and his celebration of graphic artists raises questions—about the respective power of the literary, the visual, and their interactions to represent African America—that would be addressed in media well beyond interartistic texts. The second half of the twentieth century would explore the problem of word-and-image relations in a wider variety of arenas. In illustrated books, comics, movies, television, the fine arts, and other forms, the mixing of the visual and the verbal would shed light on a question of great importance to Locke: "Who and what is Negro?"[14]

What would Locke have made of the representation of civil rights and black nationalism in the images and writing associated with the Black Arts Movement's "Black Aesthetic"? How would Locke have reacted to the way ideas of black identity emerged in American popular culture, ranging from *The Cosby Show* to Cedric the Entertainer to videos on MTV? Would Locke have maintained his faith in the visual if he'd been able to see Aaron MacGruder's *Boondocks* comic strip or Glenn Ligon's text paintings (which display the words of African American writers repeatedly stenciled on a white ground) or Kara Walker's large-scale black-and-white silhouettes of slaves in her work *The End of Uncle Tom?* Would he have claimed these artists, writers, and performers as the latest incarnation of the New Negro, individuals whose aesthetic experimentations are married to their interest in "social documentation and criticism"? Would he have seen—in the heterogeneity and complexity of interartistic work in the second half of the twentieth century—a sense of a heterogeneous African America that undermines notions of a unitary black identity?

Locke may not have approved of some of this new interartistic work, but he certainly would have wrestled with such questions. For audiences today, he presents a model of critical engagement in African American arts and letters. His inquires into the range of African American arts and letters during the first half of the twentieth century encourage us to explore the way ideas about race inform the variety of work emerging from African American as well as non–African American writers, artists, and performers. His examination of verbal and visual forms persuades us to attend to the particularity and complexity of contemporary African American arts and letters. We may not be able to claim that today's writers and artists are direct descendants of Locke's New Negroes, but we can follow Locke in exploring how word and image and the interplay between them ask: "Who and what" is African American?

Notes · Index

Notes

Introduction

1. Eric Walrond and Miguel Covarrubias, "Enter the New Negro, a Distinctive Type Recently Created by the Coloured Cabaret Belt in New York," *Vanity Fair,* December 1924, 61.
2. Paul Kellogg to D. W. Alexander, no date. Alain Locke Papers, Box 88, Folder 4, Moorland-Spingarn Room, Howard University, Washington, D.C.
3. In previous centuries, the term "New Negro" had been used to describe Africans transplanted to the New World (1700s), the newly emancipated slave (1860s), and the politically activist African American of the 1890s–1910s. See Henry Louis Gates, "The Trope of a New Negro and the Reconstruction of the Image of the Black," in Philip Fisher, ed., *The New American Studies: Essays from Representations* (Berkeley: University of California Press, 1991); Eric Sundquist, *To Wake the Nations: Race in the Making of American Literature* (Cambridge, Mass.: Harvard University Press, 1993); Wilson Moses, *The Golden Age of Black Nationalism* (New York: Oxford University Press, 1978).
4. See Werner Sollors, "Ethnic Modernism," in Sacvan Berkovitch, ed., *The Cambridge History of American Literature,* Vol. 6: *Prose Writing, 1910–1950* (Cambridge: Cambridge University Press, 2003), 510–511.
5. Imagism was a literary movement of the 1910s. Ezra Pound, Amy Lowell, and other Imagist poets believed that poetry should employ striking and extremely concise visual images.
6. Wendy Steiner, *The Color of Rhetoric* (Chicago: University of Chicago Press, 1982), xi.

7. W. J. T. Mitchell, *Picture Theory* (Chicago: University of Chicago Press, 1994), 94, 95.
8. Ibid., 94.
9. Samuel A. Floyd Jr., "On Integrative Inquiry," *Lenox Avenue: A Journal of Interartistic Inquiry,* 1 (1995), 5.
10. Samuel A. Floyd, Jr., "Editor's Preface," ibid., 1; and Jeffrey Magee, "Report on the Integrative Studies Retreat," *Lenox Avenue: A Journal of Interartistic Inquiry,* 2 (1996), 4.
11. Mitchell, *Picture Theory,* 89–90.

1. Exit the Old Negro

1. Eric Walrond and Miguel Covarrubias, "Enter the New Negro, a Distinctive Type Recently Created by the Coloured Cabaret Belt in New York," *Vanity Fair,* December 1924, 61; Alain Locke, "Enter the New Negro," *Survey Graphic,* 6, no. 6 (March 1925), 631.
2. Locke, "Enter the New Negro," 631.
3. See Henry Louis Gates Jr., "The Trope of a New Negro and the Reconstruction of the Image of the Black," in Philip Fisher, ed., *The New American Studies* (Berkeley: University of California Press, 1991); Eric Sundquist, *To Wake the Nations: Race in the Making of American Literature* (Cambridge, Mass.: Harvard University Press, 1993).
4. Reprinted in Gates, "The Trope of a New Negro," 324.
5. Booker T. Washington, *A New Negro for a New Century* (New York: Arno, 1969; orig. pub. 1900).
6. Gates, "The Trope of a New Negro," 327, Washington, *A New Negro,* 3.
7. Gates, "The Trope of a New Negro," 326–327.
8. Alain Locke, "Youth Speaks," in *Survey Graphic,* 6, no. 6 (March 1925), 659.
9. William Stanley Braithwaite, "The Negro in American Literature" (1924), reprinted in Cary Wintz, ed., *The Critics and the Harlem Renaissance* (New York: Garland, 1996). Braithwaite wrote: "All that was accomplished between Phillis Wheatley and Paul Laurence Dunbar, considered by critical standards, is negligible, and of historical interest only" (17).
10. Braithwaite, "The Negro in American Literature," 11.
11. One exception was Sterling Brown, who published *The Negro in American Fiction* in 1937. His work was a more comprehensive account.
12. See W. E. B. Du Bois, "The Negro in Literature and Art," *Annals of the American Academy of Political and Social Sciences* (1913): "The expression in words of the tragic experience of the Negro race is to be found in various places. First, of course, there are those, like Harriet Beecher Stowe, who wrote from without the race" (reprinted in Cary Wintz, ed., *The Emergence of the Harlem Renaissance* [New York: Garland, 1996], 3). Sterling Brown lists a number of other writers, including Mrs. M. V. Victor, whose *Maum Guineas' Children* (1861), Brown claims, was more popular than *Uncle*

Tom's Cabin among Union soldiers. Sterling Brown, *The Negro in American Fiction* (New York: Atheneum, 1978; orig. pub. 1937), 42.

13. Locke, "Enter the New Negro," 631.

14. Braithwaite, "The Negro in American Literature," 12.

15. In 2002, the New-York Historical Society presented a show in honor of the 150th anniversary of the publication of *Uncle Tom's Cabin*. The show exhibited a number of illustrated texts, Uncle Tom board games, Topsy dolls, trading cards, advertisements, Italian ceramics, and French porcelain, among other objects. See also Marcus Wood, *Blind Memory* (New York: Routledge, 2000).

16. Benjamin Brawley, "The Negro in American Fiction" (1923), reprinted in Wintz, *The Critics and the Harlem Renaissance*, 25.

17. Sundquist, *To Wake the Nations*, 336–338. See also Michael North, *The Dialect of Modernism: Race, Language, and Twentieth-Century Literature* (New York: Oxford University Press, 1994).

18. George Washington Cable, *The Grandissimes* (New York: Scribner's, 1899), 245.

19. Thomas Nelson Page, "Marse Chan," in Page, *In Ole Virginia, or "Marse Chan" and Other Stories* (New York: Scribner's, 1904), 10.

20. Thomas Nelson Page, *Red Rock* (New York: Scribner's, 1902), 92.

21. Ibid., 358–360.

22. Thomas Dixon, *The Leopard's Spots* (New York: Doubleday, Page, 1903), 5.

23. Ibid., 93.

24. Braithwaite, "The Negro in American Literature," 14.

25. Brawley, "The Negro in American Fiction," 27.

26. See Octavus Roy Cohen, *Bigger and Blacker* (Boston: Little Brown, 1925).

27. Emmett J. Scott, review of Haldane Macfall, *The Wooings of Jezebel Pettyfer* (New York: Knopf, 1925).

28. Braithwaite, "The Negro in American Literature," 13.

29. See Daniel Boorstin, *The Image* (New York: Vintage, 1992), 13.

30. Walter Benjamin, "The Work of Art in the Age of Its Technological Reproducibility," trans. Edmund Jephcott and Harry Zohn, in Walter Benjamin, *Selected Writings, Volume 3: 1935–1938,* ed. Howard Eiland and Michael W. Jennings (Cambridge, Mass: Harvard University Press, 2002), 218.

31. Boorstin, *The Image,* 13.

32. Judy Larson, *American Illustration: Romance, Adventure, and Suspense* (Chicago: University of Chicago Press, 1986); Francis John Martin, "The Image of Black People in American Illustration from 1825 to 1925" (Ph.D. diss., UCLA, 1986), 473.

33. Gates, "The Trope of a New Negro," 339.

34. See Richard Ohmann, *Selling Culture: Magazines, Markets, and Class at the Turn of the Century* (New York: Verso, 1998); and Joseph Boskin, *Sambo: The Rise and Demise of an American Jester* (New York: Oxford University Press, 1986).

35. The lithographs presented the great men of the era: Frederick Douglass (the

leader of African America), Robert Brown Elliott and J. H. Rainey (former members of Congress), Blanche K. Bruce (an ex-senator), William Wells Brown (author of *Clotel, or the President's Daughter*), Richard Greener (dean of Howard University), Richard Allen (first bishop of the African Methodist Episcopal Church), Henry Highland Garnet (the great orator), P. B. S. Pinchback (former governor of Louisiana and grandfather of Jean Toomer), and others. They are in the Prints and Photographs Collection at the Library of Congress.

36. Martin, "The Image of Black People in American Illustration," 402.

37. Bryan F. Le Beau, *Currier and Ives: America Imagined* (Washington, D.C.: Smithsonian Institution Press, 2001), 231.

38. Braithwaite, "The Negro in American Literature," 14–15.

39. Scott, review of Haldane Macfall, *The Wooings of Jezebel Pettyfer,* 33.

40. James A. Porter, *Modern Negro Art* (New York: Dryden, 1943), 82–83.

41. E. W. Kemble, "Illustrating *Huckleberry Finn,*" *Colophon: A Book Collectors' Quarterly* (February 1930), posted at http://etext.lib.virginia.edu/railton/huckfinn/colophon.html.

42. Martin, "The Image of Black People in American Illustration," 473.

43. Kemble also illustrated the work of E. K. Means and Ruth McHenry Stuart, minor writers also mentioned by critics.

44. Boskin, *Sambo,* 127. Kemble's Gold Dust Twins, used in advertisements, were extraordinarily popular images. He drew the twins—named Dusty and Goldy—to advertise Gold Dust Washing Powder. The young boys had big lips and nappy hair and were semi-nude. They were immensely popular. A Chicago publisher put out *Fairbanks's Drawing and Painting Book Showing the Gold Dust Twins at Work and Play as Sketched by the Famous E. W. Kemble* in 1904, and the twins appeared on the soap powder packaging for almost seventy-five years. See Boskin, *Sambo,* 140–141.

45. Braithwaite, "The Negro in American Literature," 11.

46. See George Frederickson, *The Black Image in the White Mind: The Debate on Afro-American Character and Destiny, 1817–1914* (Hanover, N.H.: Wesleyan University Press, 1971), 110–129, 216–222, 279.

47. Frederickson, *The Black Image in the White Mind,* 280.

48. Brawley, "The Negro in American Fiction," 25.

49. Alain Locke, "American Literary Tradition and the Negro," *Modern Quarterly,* 3 (May–June 1926), 220.

50. Alain Locke, *Negro Art: Past and Present* (Washington, D.C.: Associates in Negro Folk Education, 1936), 9.

51. Brown, *The Negro in American Fiction,* 1–2.

52. See Richard Brilliant, *Portraiture* (Cambridge, Mass.: Harvard University Press, 1991), 7–9.

53. Werner Sollors, "Was Roxy Black?" in Jonathan Brennan, ed., *Mixed Race Literature* (Stanford: Stanford University Press, 2002), 74. See also Wendy Rick Reaves, *Celebrity Caricature in America* (New Haven: Yale University

Press, in association with the National Portrait Gallery, Smithsonian Institution, 1998).

54. Sander Gilman, *Difference and Pathology: Stereotypes of Sexuality, Race, and Madness* (Ithaca: Cornell University Press, 1985), 17–18.

55. E. H. Gombrich, *Art and Illusion* (Princeton: Princeton University Press, 2000), 85, 87.

56. Gilman, *Difference and Pathology,* 26.

57. Sollors, "Was Roxy Black?" 74–75.

58. Gombrich, *Art and Illusion,* 344–345, 353.

59. Locke, "American Literary Tradition and the Negro," 220.

60. According to the *Oxford English Dictionary,* a chromograph is "an apparatus for multiplying copies of written matter, in which aniline dye is used instead of ink. The writing is transferred to the surface of a gelatinous substance, whence many copies can be taken on paper by pressure, without further application of the pigment."

61. Sollors, "Was Roxy Black?" 74.

62. Harriet Beecher Stowe, *Uncle Tom's Cabin, or Life among the Lowly* (Cambridge, Mass.: Riverside, 1892), vol. 2, 369.

63. Ibid., vol. 1, 221.

64. Ibid., vol. 1, 247.

65. Joel Chandler Harris, *The Complete Tales of Uncle Remus* (Boston: Houghton Mifflin, 1983), xxi.

66. Ibid., xxvii.

67. Quoted in Frederickson, *The Black Image in the White Mind,* 280.

68. Kemble, "Illustrating *Huckleberry Finn.*"

69. Joel Chandler Harris, quoted in Martin, "The Image of Black People in American Illustration," 461.

70. Droch, "Family Pride, or Art for Life's Sake," *Life Magazine,* 28 (December 1896), 477, quoted in Martin, "The Image of Black People in American Illustration," 501.

71. Sollors, "Was Roxy Black?" 74. J. Hillis Miller, *Illustration* (Cambridge, Mass.: Harvard University Press, 1992), 61. In recent years especially, scholars have examined the meaning of this sense of "illumination." Readers assume that there is a "normal" relation between image and text, which, as W. J. T. Mitchell writes, involves "traditional formulas involving the clear subordination and suturing of one medium to the other, often with a straightforward division of labor." Yet illustrated texts often deviate from this norm. Mitchell points to the work of Blake, in which the relation of word and image can range from the "absolutely disjunctive ('illustrations' that have no textual reference) to the absolutely synthetic identification of verbal and visual codes (marks that collapse the distinction between writing and drawing)." The illuminating effect of illustrations can vary widely, according to Mitchell's reading. W. J. T. Mitchell, *Picture Theory* (Chicago: University of Chicago Press, 1994), 91.

72. Sollors, "Was Roxy Black?" 75.
73. Miller, *Illustration*, 61.
74. See James Olney, "'I Was Born': Slave Narratives, Their Status as Literature and as Autobiography," in Charles T. Davis and Henry Louis Gates Jr., eds., *The Slave's Narrative* (New York: Oxford University Press, 1985), 151–155.
75. Oliver Wendell Holmes, "The Stereoscope and the Stereograph," *Atlantic Monthly* (1859), reprinted in Alan Trachtenberg, ed., *Classic Essays on Photography* (New Haven: Leete's Island Books, 1980), 73.
76. Stowe, *Uncle Tom's Cabin*, vol. 1, 32.
77. Photogravures are made by transferring a photographic negative of an image onto a metal plate. The artist then etches the image on the plate, from which prints are made.
78. Stowe, *Uncle Tom's Cabin*, vol. 1, 29–30.
79. Jan Nederveen Pieterse, *White on Black: Images of Africa and Blacks in Western Popular Culture* (New Haven: Yale University Press, 1992), 155.
80. Gilman, *Difference and Pathology*, 20.
81. Walter Lippmann, *Public Opinion* (New York: Free Press, 1997), 54–55.
82. Ibid., 60–61.
83. Charles S. Johnson, "Public Opinion and the Negro," *Opportunity* (July 1923), 202.
84. Ibid.
85. Ibid.
86. Locke, "Enter the New Negro," 631.

2. Enter the New Negro

1. Although scholars of the Harlem Renaissance tend to focus on Alain Locke, Richard Robbins, in his book *Sidelines Activist*, persuasively argues that Charles S. Johnson was one of three "midwives" of the movement (Robbins includes Locke and Jessie Fauset in this category). Robbins quotes Johnson as saying that Locke was "cast in a role merely of press agent." In addition, he argues that Locke acted as the literary and artistic critic, while Johnson organized projects, published, and disseminated the work of black writers and artists. Richard Robbins, *Sidelines Activist: Charles S. Johnson and the Struggle for Civil Rights* (Jackson: University Press of Mississippi, 1996), 54–55.
2. Charles S. Johnson to Locke, March 4, 1924, Alain Locke Papers, Box 40, Folder 25, Moorland-Spingarn Room, Howard University.
3. Locke's coronation as the steward of the "New Negro" movement was no sudden change of fortune. An extraordinarily well-educated scholar, Locke graduated from Harvard University magna cum laude and Phi Beta Kappa in 1907; he then attended Oxford as a Rhodes scholar. Upon his return to the United States in 1912, he taught philosophy at Howard University and encouraged a generation of bright, young students in their scholarly and literary endeavors. In 1916, Locke returned to Harvard to complete his doctoral

dissertation, "Problems of Classification in Theory of Value," after which he again taught at Howard. Steven Watson, *The Harlem Renaissance* (New York: Pantheon, 1995), 24.

4. A number of other prominent individuals attended, including Albert Barnes, John Dewey, Zona Gale, Horace Liveright, T. E. Stribling, and Clement Wood. See George Hutchinson, *The Harlem Renaissance in Black and White* (Cambridge, Mass.: Harvard University Press, 1995), 389–390, on the history of the dinner and the importance of generational conflict among the participants.

5. A former French teacher and a graduate of Cornell University, Fauset came to the *Crisis* after a starting a long correspondence with Du Bois in 1903, following the publication of Du Bois's book *The Souls of Black Folk*. See Watson, *The Harlem Renaissance*, 19–20.

6. David Levering Lewis, *When Harlem Was in Vogue* (New York: Oxford University Press, 1981), 93.

7. *Survey Graphic*, 6, no. 6 (March 1925), 626–627.

8. The visual language of Kellogg's statement is striking; he recognizes the inadequacy of earlier forms of literal and figurative visualizations of African America and calls for something appropriate for these "new northern communities." Paul Kellogg to D. W. Alexander, no date. Locke Papers, Box 88, Folder 4.

9. *Survey Graphic*, 6, no. 6 (March 1925), 627; Lewis, *When Harlem Was in Vogue*, 115.

10. Leon Whipple, "Letters and Life," *Survey Graphic*, 56, no. 9 (August 1, 1926), 517.

11. The texts have received a great deal of critical attention since their publication. Yet there has been little discussion about a central part of the works: the presence and logic of the textual and the visual throughout each. A welcome exception is the work of George Hutchinson, who writes about the *Survey Graphic* and *The New Negro* in his book *The Harlem Renaissance in Black and White*. He does not, however, address the two printings of the anthology.

12. The simplest way of distinguishing between the two printings is by looking at the number of pages. The 1925 edition contains 446 pages; the 1927 edition has 452 pages. The reason for the increase was that Locke added to the bibliography at the conclusion of the text. Other differences that did not affect the size of the volume were more important. The table of contents of the 1927 edition reflects most of these changes, though it contains some mistakes. For example, Miguel Covarrubias' drawing *Jazz* remains listed (though deleted from the book), and a bronze mask from the Guillaume collection has the wrong page number. (Paul Guillaume [1891–1934] was a prominent French art dealer. He collected not only African art but also modern sculpture and painting.) These are unimportant differences, probably the result of copyediting errors. Post–Harlem Renaissance reprintings of the anthology have used both printings without any commentary. The following presses used the 1925 version of *The New Negro*: Arno, 1968; Johnson Reprint Corporation,

1968; Ayer, 1986. The following presses used the 1927 version of *The New Negro:* Atheneum, 1967, 1968, 1970, 1974, 1983, 1986, 1992; Simon and Schuster, 1992, 1997. The confusion about the printings is widespread. Simon and Schuster used the second printing of the anthology as the basis for the 1992 reprint. Though Arnold Rampersad, in his introduction to that reprint, described the importance of the Winold Reiss drawings, Simon and Schuster did not include them in the volume. When I called Simon and Schuster in 1999 to ask about their decision to use the 1927 printing, I was told by an assistant editor, who did not know about the two different versions, that the reasons were probably financial. The many reprintings have contributed to the confusion about the two editions. Even the Library of Congress has miscatalogued them. Yale University's Beinecke Library, however, correctly identifies the two different printings.

13. Alain Locke, *Negro Art: Past and Present* (Washington, D.C.: Associates in Negro Folk Education, 1936), 9.

14. In his review of *The New Negro,* in *Opportunity,* 4 (February 1926), Robert Bagnall complained about the omnipresence of Locke's writing in the volume. "There is, however, one glaring fault in this book which we cannot overlook. It is the frequency with which the editor, Mr. Locke, obtrudes himself upon the scene. Five times he appears before its footlights, reminding one of those chairmen who must make a new speech every time he introduces a new speaker."

15. Alain Locke, "Harlem," *Survey Graphic,* 6, no. 6 (March 1925), 629–630.

16. Alain Locke, "Enter the New Negro," *Survey Graphic,* ibid., 633.

17. Locke, "Harlem," 630.

18. Ibid., 631–634.

19. For a history of the magazine, see Clarke A. Chambers, *Paul U. Kellogg and the Survey: Voices for Social Welfare and Social Justice* (Minneapolis: University of Minnesota Press, 1971).

20. Ibid., 36, 53. The Kellogg brothers commissioned prominent artists Lewis Hine and Joseph Stella to provide photographs and sketches of immigrants for the magazine. Hine was one of the fathers of documentary photography; he traveled the country, taking photographs of immigrants, child laborers, tenements, and sweatshops. Many of his photographs were used as evidence to encourage reform legislation. Stella was a painter who depicted scenes from the immigrant neighborhood of the Lower East Side of New York. Using a naturalistic style, he drew Ellis Island immigrants, mining disasters, and the mining areas of West Virginia and Pittsburgh as though he were attempting to record, almost photographically, images of individuals. (Stella later came to embrace the principles of Futurism, an aesthetic movement in painting and literature which was founded in Italy and whose aim was to represent the speed, noise, and disorder of the machine age. Stella's work for the *Survey* during his time there, however, was in a naturalistic vein (*Phaidon Dictionary of Twentieth-Century Art* [New York: Phaidon, 1973], 368).

21. Chambers, *Paul U. Kellogg and the Survey,* 84.

22. Ibid., 104–110.
23. Ibid., 53. See Alan Trachtenberg, *Reading American Photographs: Images as History from Matthew Brady to Walker Evans* (New York: Hill and Wang, 1989), 195.
24. Chambers, *Paul U. Kellogg and the Survey,* 112.
25. The New Negro issue is perhaps most similar to the Mexico issue, which contained polemical, historical, and sociological essays, one poem, and reproductions of works by Diego Rivera. It also included "Mexican Types," a series of four drawings of racial types (one labeled "A Pure Aztec Type") by Winold Reiss. *Survey Graphic,* 2, no. 3 (May 1, 1924).
26. The opening commentary in the New Negro issue made this connection clear: "There are times when these forces [of 'race growth and interaction'] that work so slowly seem to flower—and we become aware that the curtain has lifted on a new act in the drama of part or all of us. Such, we believe, was the case with Ireland on the threshold of political emancipation, and the New Ireland spoke for itself in our issue of November 1921; with the New Russia which was to some degree interpreted in March 1923; and with the newly awakened Mexico, in May 1924. If *The Survey* reads the signs aright, such a dramatic flowering of a new race spirit is taking place close at home—among American Negroes, and the stage of that new episode is Harlem." *Survey Graphic,* 6, no. 6 (March 1925), 625.
27. Other magazines, such as the *Crisis,* included visual material. However, even when the table of contents listed a story or poem as "illustrated," it meant that a photo of the author appeared before the work in the body of the magazine. In the October 1925 issue of the *Crisis,* a posed photograph of Rudolph Fisher appeared before his story "High Yaller." Below the photograph was a biographical caption. Clearly, then, photographic portraits—"illustrations," in the parlance of the *Crisis*—were strictly informative. *Crisis,* 29, no. 11 (October 1925).
28. James Weldon Johnson, "The Making of Harlem," *Survey Graphic,* 6, no. 6 (March 1925), 635.
29. Ibid., 638–639.
30. Johnson concludes his piece with a statement reminiscent of Locke's earlier essay. Asserting that Negroes are full citizens of American or, more important, New York, he writes, "A thousand Negroes from Mississippi put to work as a gang in a Pittsburgh steel mill will for a long time remain a thousand Negroes from Mississippi. Under the conditions that prevail in New York they would all within six months become New Yorkers. The rapidity with which Negroes become good New Yorkers is one of the marvels to observe." Ibid., 639.
31. Charles S. Johnson, "Black Workers and the City," *Survey Graphic,* 6, no. 6 (March 1925), 719. The New York City draft riots occurred in July 1863. Mobs (predominantly Irish and Catholic workers), enraged about the first national draft during the Civil War, destroyed property, closed the city's businesses, and attacked New York's black population.

32. Ibid., 641.

33. Johnson distinguishes the Negro "type" from the Jew because of their different environments. The Negro's "metier is agriculture," while the Jew is "by every aptitude and economic attachment a city dweller." Johnson, "Black Workers and the City," 641.

34. Johnson also writes that the "city Negro is only now in evolution," changing in individual and group relations, in the reorganization of life, in relation to whites and to religion. Ibid., 642–643.

35. Mahonri Young was a sculptor and painter best known for his depictions of religious subjects, boxers, and laborers. Born in Salt Lake City (he was the grandson of Brigham Young), he studied in New York and Paris in the early decades of the twentieth century.

36. A very different sort of illustration accompanied an article Johnson wrote for the April 15, 1928, issue of the *Survey*. The article, entitled "Negro Workers and the Unions," continues the subject of Johnson's piece in the New Negro issue. The illustration by African American artist Aaron Douglas creates a different effect, however, and suggests that the typifying, figurative tradition of Young's drawing undermined Johnson's notions of racial heterogeneity. Douglas' piece is a figure in profile; the body is indicated by a solid block of black and is surrounded by black shapes that appear to be vegetation. A curving streak of black recedes in the lower left corner, suggesting a road. The Douglas figure seems strong and powerful because its uniform blackness dominates the page and has the same black monotone of the other shapes. With its black-and-white color scheme and hard lines, it acts not as an illustration but rather as a complement to the article. Rather than referring directly to elements of the article, it provides an additional view onto "Negro workers." Moreover, because the drawing is situated in the middle of the article, it becomes the focal point of the page. But although it is a study of shape, line, and contrast rather than a likeness of an individual, it indicates the impossibility of claiming a single, veritable type. The drawing suggests a loose pattern (with the black-and-white shapes) that the mass of Negro workers may follow. The abstraction of the drawing calls attention to the artificiality of types. This illustration opens up the racial aesthetics of the New Negro. While the subjects of the two articles are the same, the changes in the illustrations suggest a move beyond conventional, figurative portrayals to depictions of multifaceted African American identity. Although both illustrations refer to the rhetoric of types, the typicality of the Young drawing echoes the long figurative tradition that sometimes embraced stereotype because it allowed for a reading of racial homogeneity. The Douglas illustration avoids the danger of stereotype because it employs a visual language that was not historically suspect, according to theoreticians such as Locke. It claims not racial homogeneity but a concern for the social status of the black worker in general.

37. Locke Papers, Box 88, Folder 5.

38. Alain Locke, "To Certain of Our Philistines," *Opportunity*, 3 (May 1925), 155.

39. Ibid.

40. During his tenure as editor of the *Survey*, Paul Kellogg also commissioned artists such as Diego Rivera and José Orozco to present folk themes. Rivera and Orozco were prominent Mexican painters who documented folk culture; both their subjects and the idioms in which they painted evolved from Mexican folk culture. Rivera and Orozco, who were involved in the Mexican Revolution, employed poster-like compositions of flat forms and vibrant colors to portray historical moments and social conditions in Mexico at that time. This technique was known as "expressive Realism." Although the work of both had Cubist strains, the work would profoundly influence the American Realist school. *Phaidon Dictionary*, 287, 320–321.

41. Locke writes that Reiss expresses his interpretations both "concretely in his portrait sketches" and "abstractly in his symbolic designs." Locke identifies Reiss's more realistic drawings *and* his more abstract drawings as serving to portray African Americans. Alain Locke, introduction to Winold Reiss, "Harlem Types," *Survey Graphic*, 6, no. 6 (March 1925), 651–653.

42. Reiss felt the allure of the United States and, in 1913, left Germany for financial and political reasons. Reiss had married Henrietta Lüthy in 1912; she became pregnant in 1913. Reiss thought that the opportunities for work would be great in the United States. In addition, Jeffrey Stewart argues, the rise of German militarism due to Kaiser Wilhelm's *Weltpolitik* prompted Reiss, born to a pacifist family, to relocate. (Jeffrey Stewart, *To Color America* [Washington, D.C.: Smithsonian Institution Press, 1989], 25–26.) Just as important, however, was Reiss's interest in visiting and depicting Native American tribes. As a child, Reiss had read the "Wild West" novels of the German author Karl May and the frontier novels of James Fenimore Cooper. Stewart describes the "Coopermania" that ran through Germany during the 1890s, when Reiss was a boy (ibid., 21). Reiss did not embark immediately on his quest. Settling in New York, he soon found work, designing covers for *Scribner's*, illustrating *Mother Goose Rhymes Done in Poster Stamps*, and designing a "modernist" interior for the Busy Lady Bakery, all in 1915 (ibid., 28). After spending the duration of World War I teaching and working in New York, Reiss traveled to Montana to do drawings of the Blackfeet tribe. In 1920, he traveled to Mexico and later, in 1922, returned to Europe for a brief visit.

43. Franz von Stuck was a Bavarian artist and founding member of the Munich Secession, a group of artists who broke with the Künstlergenossenschaft (the Munich Artists' Association) in 1893. See Maria Makela, *The Munich Secession: Art and Artists in Turn-of-the-Century Munich* (Princeton: Princeton University Press, 1990), 104–113.

44. According to Jeffrey Stewart, German artists studied African art and the work of ethnologists and travel writers of that era, including Leo Frobenius,

Karl von den Steinern, and Eduard Pecheul-Loesche. Stewart, *To Color America*, 23.

45. *Phaidon Dictionary*, 274; Stewart, *To Color America*, 44. Other practitioners of the Neue Sachlichkeit were George Grosz and Otto Dix. G. F. Hartlaub coined the term in 1923, to describe an exhibition of postwar painting at the Kunsthalle in Mannheim.

46. Reiss was not engaged in this work, for commercial reasons. Reiss wrote to Locke: "I have to tell you again how much I liked to work with you and I only wish that we will have once an occasion in which we can prove just for all our ideals regardless of commercial people." Reiss to Locke, December 31, 1925, Locke Papers, Box 79, Folder 57.

47. Locke, introduction to Reiss, "Harlem Types," 651.

48. Ibid., 653.

49. Ibid., 652.

50. This image, which seems to play with ideas of African American primitivism in the context of the 1920s, seems prescient. Congo's afro and direct gaze could easily be elements of a late 1960s or early 1970s portrait of, say, a Black Panther or a black performer.

51. The *Crisis* also published portraits of individuals in almost all of its issues during the 1920s. As in the *Survey Graphic*, the portraits were of residents of Harlem and other areas. Unlike the New Negro issue, the *Crisis* used photographs of individuals to document their achievements. Baby portraits, graduation photos, and similar images filled the pages, along with names, dates, and other information.

52. It is interesting to note that, according to the captions, these are middle-class individuals: a woman lawyer, a college student, a Boy Scout. "Congo" is the exception.

53. Reiss, "Harlem Types," 652–654.

54. See Jo-Anne Birnie Danzker, *Franz von Stuck: Die Sammlung Des Museums Villa Stuck* (Munich: Minerva, 1997), 100–101, for an example of the process von Stuck employed. See also Danzker, *Franz von Stuck und die Photographie* (Munich: Prestel, 1996); and Makela, *The Munich Secession*, 74. I am indebted to Werner Sollors for pointing out this connection.

55. Alain Locke, *Negro Art: Past and Present* (New York: Associates in Negro Folk Education, 1936), 51.

56. Harold Jackman, an intimate of Countee Cullen, was the model for *A College Lad*. That the portrait of Jackman is identified not by name but by status is evidence of the *Survey Graphic*'s interest in types, rather than in representative individuals.

57. Sarah Merrill to Locke, February 10, 1925, Locke Papers, Box 88, Folder 17.

58. Locke, "Harlem," 630.

59. Locke, *Negro Art*, 38.

60. Locke, "Enter the New Negro," 631.

61. Locke, *Negro Art*, 70.

62. There was quite a debate about the cover during the production of the maga-

zine. Although Locke admired both the design and the portrait, he initially resisted the layout because he felt that the images would clash. He and editor Merrill complained about it to Kellogg, but Kellogg relied on the advice of the sales people to help the advertising of the magazine (Paul Kellogg to Locke, February 17, 1925, Locke Papers, Box 88, Folder 7). On February 5, 1925, Kellogg sent a telegram to Locke: "Sales and advertising experts say we can double sales of Harlem number if we use reis marvelous head Roland Hayes on cover also inside. More sales more educational reach more-over Hayes personifies youth, racial genius new Negro as nothing else please wire him urging him grant this permission" (Locke Papers, Box 88, Folder 5). Hayes left the decision up to Locke, and Reiss approved the layout (Paul Kellogg to Locke, February 12, 1925, Locke Papers, Box 88, Folder 7). The confluence of Reiss's design and the Hayes portrait did produce a disconcerting effect. Although the editors recognized that the two styles might be discordant, the juxtaposition does garner attention. The blue design frames the disembodied face of Hayes in such a way that the viewer cannot help being attracted to it. The tension is tremendously engaging.

63. *Survey Graphic,* 6, no. 6 (March 1925), cover.
64. Ibid., 628.
65. Ibid., 662.
66. Claude McKay, *A Long Way from Home* (New York: Harcourt, Brace, Jovanovich, 1970), 136.
67. The originals also contained swaths of pink.
68. On January 15, 1925, Kellogg wrote to Locke that Boni had called him to discuss the "republication of the materials in our Harlem number in book form." Locke Papers, Box 88, Folder 7.
69. Albert Boni to Paul Kellogg, March 20, 1925, Locke Papers, Box 88, Folder 2.
70. Locke Papers, Box 40, Folder 26.
71. Many of the decisions to include additional material in *The New Negro* were based on commercial considerations. For example, drawings by the young Mexican caricaturist Miguel Covarrubias were added at the behest of Louis Baer, who worked at Boni. Baer, who mentioned Covarrubias in at least three letters, wrote to Locke on May 19, 1925, that "everyone seems to think the Covarrubias things (or some of them, at any rate) would go very well in the book, and I will get in touch with him very shortly to find what arrangements we can make." Locke did not seem all that interested in the Covarrubias drawings, which can be easily construed as racist caricature. Unsurprisingly, he dropped two drawings for the second printing of the anthology.
72. Reiss's decorative work is an outgrowth of Jugendstil (Germany's version of France's Art Nouveau), which Reiss came to know through von Stuck. See S. Tschudi Madsen, *Art Nouveau* (New York: McGraw-Hill, 1976), 173–191.
73. In *Negro Art: Past and Present,* Locke describes Reiss's contributions: "Artistically the series, only half of which could be published in the then expensive process of color reproduction, was a great and effective revelation

not only of the range but the expressiveness of Negro types." Locke, *Negro Art*, 51.

74. The success of Locke's intention to turn *The New Negro* into a piece of art unto itself was noted by critic Robert Bagnall, who marveled at its physical beauty. In his review in *Opportunity*, 4 (February 1926), Bagnall wrote, "The cover design is striking, the type fresh and bold, the margins wide, the decorative illustrations novel, the drawings and symbolic sketches of Aaron Douglas powerful and effective, the two studies by Miguel Covarrubias startling in their animation, and the sixteen portrait studies in color by Winold Reiss, beautiful and revealing. The physical side of the book—utterly apart from its reading matter, makes the volume a valuable possession—one to be treasured."

75. See Covarrubias, *Negro Drawings* (New York: Knopf, 1927).

76. On April 13, 1925, Locke wrote to Boni about the contract with Reiss: "His drawings will do more than any other one feature to put the book over." Locke Papers, Box 122, Folder 12.

77. On June 4, 1924, Kellogg referred to a letter he had received from Locke about the *Survey Graphic*. Locke had written: "I shall make New York again June 11th as agreed upon. Could Mr. Reiss in the interim however look up a few types?" Locke Papers, Box 88, Folder 5.

78. Locke Papers, Box 40, Folder 26.

79. Locke later wrote about this decision in *Negro Art: Past and Present*. "Under such conditions [the reaction to 'Nordic color prejudice' among African American artists],—especially as it was the program of the movement of which this book was an early expression to lead a campaign of healthy-minded racialism, it was particularly necessary to have the whole interesting gamut of Negro types portrayed with even-handed objectivity, and yet not photographically. (Unless we could have had the kind of careful folk portraiture which the art photography of the late Doris Ullmann later proved was possible.)" In this statement, Locke uses the word "types" to include both type sketches and representative portraits. Locke, *Negro Art*, 50–51.

80. Elise Johnson McDougald to Locke, no date, Alain Locke Papers, Box 115, Folder 4.

81. Locke, "To Certain of Our Philistines," 155.

82. Ibid., 156. This aesthetic debate was not limited to Locke; Douglas likewise commented on the controversy surrounding Reiss's drawings. He described what he thought was missing in understandings of African American beauty and art. In a letter to his fiancée, Alta Sawyer, Douglas wrote glowingly of Reiss's drawings. Like Locke, he rejected "white" standards of beauty, and applauded Reiss for creating real art that was not subject to the whims of the public. Douglas to Alta Sawyer, no date, Aaron Douglas Papers, New York Public Library, Schomburg Center for Research in Black Culture, Box 1, Folder 1, Letter 2.

83. Albert Barnes was a medical doctor and successful businessman. He was an

avid art collector who was especially interested in African American culture. In 1922, he founded the Barnes Foundation to promote arts education and the appreciation of art.

84. Alain Locke, "Negro Youth Speaks," in Locke, *The New Negro, 50.*
85. Ibid.
86. Albert Barnes, "Negro Art in America," in Locke, *The New Negro, 19.*
87. Ibid., 19–20.
88. Braithwaite, "The Negro in American Literature," in Locke, *The New Negro, 42.*
89. Locke, *Negro Art, 11.*
90. Alain Locke, "The Legacy of the Ancestral Arts," in Locke, *The New Negro, 254.*
91. Ibid., 256.
92. Ibid., 267.
93. Ibid., 262.
94. In *Negro Art,* Locke wrote: "It is, thus, an African influence at second remove upon our younger Negro modernistic painters and sculptors; in being modernistic, they are indirectly being African" (70).
95. Ibid., 51, 70.
96. Quoted in Amy Kirschke, *Aaron Douglas: Art, Race, and the Harlem Renaissance* (Jackson: University Press of Mississippi, 1995), 13.
97. Aaron Douglas to Alta Sawyer, no date, Aaron Douglas Papers, Box 1, Folder 8, Letter 81.
98. See Douglas to Alta Sawyer, Douglas Papers, Box 1, Folder 2, Letter 20.
99. See Douglas to Alta Sawyer, no date, Douglas Papers, Box 1, Folder 8, Letter 81.
100. Douglas wrote to his fiancée, Alta Sawyer, about how highly he thought of Reiss and how excited he was to work with the older artist. Douglas to Alta Sawyer, Douglas Papers, Box 1, Folder 5, Letter 43.
101. Kirschke, *Aaron Douglas, 28.*
102. Ibid., 36; Stewart, *To Color America, 61.* The Congo Room was a nightclub located in the Hotel Almanac at Broadway and West 70th Street. Club Ebony was also a New York nightclub, which opened in 1927.
103. Douglas to Alta Sawyer, Douglas Papers, Box 1, Folder 1, Letter 5.
104. On May 21, 1925, Paul Kellogg wrote to Locke about Elise McDougald's "suggestion to . . . include, if possible, work by Negro artists in the new book." Locke Papers, Box 88, Folder 7.
105. This technique probably emanates from Douglas' familiarity with Cubism.
106. Alain Locke to Albert and Charles Boni, March 23, 1926, Locke Papers, Box 122, Folder 22.
107. Arthur Huff Fauset was an anthropologist and author of *For Freedom: A Biographical Story of the American Negro* (1927) and *Black Gods of the Metropolis: Negro Religious Cults in the Urban North* (1944). He was Jessie Redmond Fauset's younger brother.

3. Fy-ah

1. W. E. B. Du Bois, "A Questionnaire," *Crisis,* 31 (February 1926), 165, reprinted in Cary Wintz, ed., *The Critics and the Harlem Renaissance* (New York: Garland, 1996), 347.

2. Du Bois wrote, "Most writers have said naturally that any portrayal of any kind of Negro was permissible so long as the work was pleasing and the artist sincere. But the Negro has objected vehemently—first in general to the conventional Negro in American literature; then in specific cases: to the Negro portrayed in *The Birth of a Nation;* in Macfall's *Wooings of Jezebel Pettyfer* and in Stribling's *Birthright;* in Octavius [sic] Roy Cohen's monstrosities. In general they have contended that while the individual portrait may be true and artistic, the net result to American literature to date is to picture twelve million Americans as prostitutes, thieves and fools and that such 'freedom' in art is miserably unfair." Ibid.

3. Ibid.

4. Langston Hughes, "The Negro in Art: How Shall He Be Portrayed—A Symposium," *Crisis,* 31 (February 1926), 165, reprinted in Wintz, *The Critics and the Harlem Renaissance,* 351.

5. See Steven Watson, *The Harlem Renaissance: Hub of African American Culture* (New York: Pantheon, 1995) 16–27.

6. Quoted in Cary Wintz, *Black Culture and the Harlem Renaissance* (College Station: Texas A&M University Press, 1996; orig. pub. 1988), 123.

7. W. E. B. Du Bois, "Criteria of Negro Art," *Crisis* (October 1926), 296.

8. See Abby Arthur Johnson and Ronald Maberry Johnson, *Propaganda and Aesthetics: The Literary Politics of African-American Magazines in the Twentieth Century* (Amherst: University of Massachusetts Press, 1991; orig. pub. 1979), 31–64.

9. Langston Hughes, *The Big Sea* (New York: Thunder's Mouth Press, 1986; reprint of 1940 edition), 234.

10. Mae Gwendolyn Henderson, "Portrait of Wallace Thurman," in Arna Bontemps, ed., *The Harlem Renaissance Remembered* (New York: Dodd, Mead, 1972), 149.

11. Wallace Thurman, "A Thrush at Eve with an Atavistic Wound" (review of *Flight,* by Walter White), *Messenger,* 8, no. 5 (May 1926), 154.

12. In a review, Locke wrote: "The *Little Review, This Quarter,* and the *Quill* are obvious artistic cousins." Alain Locke, review entitled "*Fire:* A Negro Magazine," *Survey: Midmonthly Number,* 58, nos. 10–12 (August 15–September 15, 1927), 563. Hughes likewise made this connection, when he reflected on the failure of *Fire!!* to last more than one issue: "That taught me a lesson about little magazines. But since white folks had them, we Negroes thought we could have one, too. But we didn't have the money." Hughes, *The Big Sea,* 238.

13. Locke, "*Fire:* A Negro Magazine," 563.

14. There were a number of "secessions" beginning in the 1890s. Munich, Vi-

enna, and Berlin all saw secession movements, in which younger artists broke away from the academies of their elders. The secession to which the *Fire!!* coterie's efforts were most akin was the Munich Secession. See *Phaidon Dictionary of Twentieth-Century Art* (New York: Phaidon, 1973), s.v. "Secession."

15. Alain Locke, "*Fire*: A Negro Magazine," 563.
16. Wallace Thurman, Editorial, *Harlem: A Forum of Negro Life,* 1, no. 1 (November 1928), reprinted in Cary Wintz, ed., *Black Writers Interpret the Harlem Renaissance* (New York: Garland, 1996), 73.
17. Ibid.
18. Wallace Thurman, "Nephews of Uncle Remus," *Independent,* 119, no. 4034 (September 1927), 296.
19. Thurman, Editorial, 73.
20. Wallace Thurman, "Negro Artists and the Negro," *New Republic,* August 31, 1927.
21. Ibid.
22. Thurman, "Fire Burns," *Fire!! Devoted to Younger Negro Artists,* 1, no. 1 (November 1926), 48.
23. Thurman, "Negro Artists and the Negro," 37.
24. Thurman, Editorial, 73.
25. Locke, "*Fire*: A Negro Magazine," 563.
26. Hughes, *The Big Sea,* 236.
27. The manifesto continues: "We believe that the Negro is fundamentally, essentially different from their Nordic neighbors. We are proud of that difference. We believe the differences to be greater spiritual endowment, greater sensitivity, greater power for artistic expression and appreciation. We believe Negro art should be trained and developed rather than capitalized and exploited. We believe finally that Negro art without Negro patrons is an impossibility. Popular American taste lacks discrimination and refinement." Quoted in Amy Kirschke, *Aaron Douglas: Art, Race, and the Harlem Renaissance* (Jackson: University Press of Mississippi, 1995), 85.
28. Foreword, *Fire!!* 1, no. 1 (November 1926).
29. Benjamin Brawley, "The Negro Literary Renaissance," *Southern Workman,* 56, no. 6 (June 1927), reprinted in Wintz, *The Critics and the Harlem Renaissance,* 58.
30. Ibid., 64.
31. Wallace Thurman, "Cordelia the Crude," *Fire!!* 1, no. 1 (November 1926), 5–6.
32. Langston Hughes, "Railroad Avenue," *Fire!!* 1, no. 1 (November 1926), 21.
33. Locke, "*Fire*: A Negro Magazine," 563.
34. Thurman, "Negro Artists and the Negro," 37.
35. Kirschke, *Aaron Douglas,* 75.
36. Richard Bruce Nugent, "Smoke, Lilies and Jade," *Fire!!* 1, no. 1 (November 1926), 33–39.
37. Ibid., 33.
38. Ibid., 37. This excerpt consists of two parts from different sections of the

story. I have eliminated a number of lines between "looking at him" and "Beauty's lips touched his."

39. Brawley, "The Negro Literary Renaissance," 58.
40. Matthew Henry, "Playing with *Fire!!* Manifesto of the Harlem Niggerati," *Griot* (Fall 1992).
41. Locke, "*Fire:* A Negro Magazine," 563.
42. Ibid.
43. Ibid.
44. As Hughes wrote, "Now *Fire* is a collector's item, and very difficult to get, being mostly ashes." Hughes, *The Big Sea,* 238.
45. Thurman, Editorial, 73.
46. Richard Bruce Nugent was disappointed with a number of aspects of the magazine, including the layout and the choice of articles and illustrations. In a letter to Dorothy Peterson (November 7, 1928), he wrote: "I suppose you have seen 'HARLEM.' . . . I was the most dissapointed individual. Do you mind running the risk of recieving obscene matter thru the mail? Because I would like to give vent to a couple of God Damns and Hells and any other cuss words you can think of. Wally could have done *so* much better with a format. The entire layout of the magazine impresses me as being nothing more than imitation of Theatre Arts Magazine. I'm not knocking just to be knocking." Beinecke Library, Yale University. I am grateful to Tom Wirth for bringing this letter to my attention.
47. Thurman, Editorial, 73–74.
48. Ibid., 74.
49. Ibid.
50. Ibid.
51. Roy de Coverly, "Holes," *Harlem,* 1, no. 1 (November 1928), reprinted in Wintz, *The Critics and the Harlem Renaissance,* 67.
52. Richard Bruce Nugent, "What Price Glory in *Uncle Tom's Cabin,*" *Harlem,* 1, no. 1 (November 1928), reprinted in Wintz, *The Critics and the Harlem Renaissance,* 77–78.
53. Wallace Thurman, "High, Low, Past and Present," *Harlem,* 1, no. 1 (November 1928), reprinted in Wintz, *The Critics and the Harlem Renaissance,* 83.
54. "Harlem Directory," *Harlem,* 1, no. 1 (November 1928), reprinted in Wintz, *The Critics and the Harlem Renaissance,* 95.
55. Ibid. The Volstead Act, otherwise known as the National Prohibition Enforcement Act, was passed in 1919 to enforce the Eighteenth Amendment, prohibiting "the manufacture, sale, or transportation of intoxicating liquors." It was repealed by the Twenty-First Amendment, which was passed in 1933.
56. Orphism was a movement in Paris in the 1910s. It advocated a style that has been described as "abstract art of color." Orphism also claimed an interchangeability of "word, image, colour, mood and medium" in its studies of light. See *Phaidon Dictionary of Twentieth-Century Art,* s.v. "Orphism."

57. Rudolph Fisher, "The City of Refuge," in Alain Locke, ed., *The New Negro: An Interpretation* (New York: Boni, 1925), 58–59.

58. Peter Szondi, *Theory of the Modern Drama* (Minneapolis: University of Minnesota Press, 1987), 48.

59. Alain Locke, "Art or Propaganda," *Harlem*, 1, no. 1 (November 1928), reprinted in Wintz, *The Critics and the Harlem Renaissance*, 64.

4. Them Big Old Lies

1. Zora Neale Hurston, *Dust Tracks on a Road* (New York: Lippincott, 1942; reprint Urbana: University of Illinois Press, 1984), 170.

2. Robert E. Hemenway, *Zora Neale Hurston: A Literary Biography* (Chicago: University of Illinois Press, 1977), 159.

3. Letter from Charlotte Osgood Mason to Miguel Covarrubias, January 21, 1935, Miguel Covarrubias Papers, Universidad de las Americas, Puebla, Mexico, Folder 199.22.

4. Robert Hemenway reports that Hurston was probably born in 1901 and that her mother died when she was nine. Hemenway, *Zora Neale Hurston*, 13.

5. Hurston, *Dust Tracks on a Road*, 174.

6. Franz Boas to Zora Neale Hurston, May 3, 1927, quoted in Hemenway, *Zora Neale Hurston*, 91.

7. Hurston had worked with Boas on measuring the physiognomies of Harlem residents in 1926. This was part of his research on the physical characteristics of races. See Hemenway, *Zora Neale Hurston*, 88.

8. Ibid., 101.

9. Ibid., 106.

10. Ibid., 109 (contract between Mason and Hurston, Dec. 8, 1927).

11. Zora Neale Hurston, *Mules and Men* (Philadelphia: Lippincott, 1935), 23.

12. Ibid., 17–18.

13. Hurston, *Dust Tracks on a Road*, 174.

14. Hurston describes hoodoo as follows: "Hoodoo, or Voodoo, as pronounced by the whites, is burning with a flame in America, with all the intensity of a suppressed religion. It has thousands of secret adherents. It adapts itself like Christianity to its locale, reclaiming some of its borrowed characteristics to itself. Such as fire-worship as signified in the Christian church by the altar and the candles. And the belief in the power of water to sanctify as in baptism. Belief in magic is older than writing. So nobody knows how it started." Hurston, *Mules and Men*, 229.

15. Henry Lee Moon, review of *Mules and Men*, in *New Republic*, December 11, 1935.

16. Alain Locke, "Deep River, Deeper Sea: Retrospective Review of the Literature of the Negro for 1935," *Opportunity*, 14 (January 1936), reprinted in Jeffrey Stewart, ed., *The Critical Temper of Alain Locke* (New York: Garland, 1983), 239.

17. H. I. Brock, review of *Mules and Men,* in *New York Times Book Review,* November 10, 1935, reprinted in Henry Louis Gates and K. A. Appiah, *Zora Neale Hurston: Critical Perspectives, Past and Present* (New York: Amistad, 1993), 14.

18. William Stanley Braithwaite, "The Negro in American Literature" (1924), reprinted in Cary Wintz, ed. *The Critics and the Harlem Renaissance* (New York: Garland, 1996), 172.

19. Franz Boas, Foreword, in Hurston, *Mules and Men,* 5.

20. Barbara Johnson, "Thresholds of Difference: Structures of Address in Zora Neale Hurston," in Gates and Appiah, *Zora Neale Hurston: Critical Perspectives,* 136.

21. Hurston, *Mules and Men,* 17.

22. Hurston, *Dust Tracks on a Road,* 175.

23. Hurston, *Mules and Men,* 89–90.

24. Ibid., 18.

25. Ibid.

26. Ibid., 18–19.

27. Ibid., 224–225.

28. Ibid., 225.

29. Ibid.

30. Hurston writes, "That is the primeval flavor of the place, and as I said before, out of this primitive approach to things, I all but lost my life. . . . Lucy really wanted to kill me. I didn't mean any harm. All I was doing was collecting songs from Slim, who used to be her man back up in West Florida before he ran off from her." Hurston, *Dust Tracks on a Road,* 185.

31. *Dust Tracks on a Road* describes the scene, emphasizing the threat to Hurston's life. Hurston writes, "Several weeks went by, then I ventured to the jook alone. Big Sweet let it be known that she was not going. But later she came in and went over to the coon-can game in the corner. . . . Big Sweet was in a crowd over in the corner, and did not see Lucy come in. But the sudden quiet of the place made her look around as Lucy charged. My friend was large and portly, but extremely light on her feet. She sprang like a lioness and I think the very surprise of Big Sweet being there when Lucy thought she was over at another party at the Pine Mill unnerved Lucy. She stopped abruptly as Big Sweet charged. The next moment, it was too late for Lucy to start again. The man who came in with Lucy tried to help her out, but two other men joined Big Sweet in the battle. It took on amazingly. It seemed that anybody who had any fighting to do, decided to settle-up then and there. Switchblades, ice-picks and old-fashioned razors were out. One or two razors had already been bent back and thrown across the room, but our fight was the main attraction." Hurston, *Dust Tracks on the Road,* 190–191.

32. Covarrubias' illustration of this fight depicts two women. They are engaged in a battle, pulling each other's hair while kicking and apparently screaming. A man holds each woman back by wrapping his arms around her and pulling. The dress of the woman on the left is white, while that of the woman on

the right has polka dots. The face of the woman on the left, framed by black, spiky hair, is presented in a three-quarters view. The face is white, to contrast with the black squinting eyes and screaming mouth. The head of the woman on the right is in profile and is completely black, suggesting a silhouette. The white of the other woman's fists contrasts strongly with her head. The two men are in silhouette, one completely in black, with an arm suggested by a sweep of black around the white dress of the woman on the left. His fingers are suggested by four black swipes against the white of the dress. The man on the left has a more conventional, silhouette face. All the figures are surrounded by a field of black that bleeds into the page around their outlines with sharp, parallel lines.

33. Hurston, *Mules and Men*, 43.
34. As a teenager, Covarrubias hung out in Los Monotes, which can be translated literally as "Big Monkeys." In the Mexican slang of the 1920s, it meant "Doodles." It was a café owned by the brother of *Survey Graphic* artist José Orozco. There, Covarrubias befriended Diego Rivera, who also provided illustrations for the *Survey*. See Adriana Williams, *Covarrubias* (Austin: University of Texas Press, 1994), 8.
35. Ibid., 40.
36. Ibid., 34. Rosa Roland was a dancer of Mexican American ancestry who employed many "ethnic" forms in her performances.
37. Mason to Covarrubias, January 21, 1935, Covarrubias Papers, Folder 199.
38. See the excellent discussion of Covarrubias' caricatures in Wendy Rick Reaves, *Celebrity Caricature in America* (New Haven: Yale University Press, in association with the National Portrait Gallery, Smithsonian Institution, 1998).
39. In a series of drawings entitled *Inclusive Tour of New York's Restaurants: A Round of Our Popular Eating places and Some Good Customers*, Covarrubias presents a variety of figures whose forms are exaggerated. "Gladys," who "lunches everyday at the soda counter," is an attenuated figure whose form suggests her loneliness and isolation. "Jerry, the Taxi Driver" is a solid figure in coat and cap who feeds coins into the automat in exchange for pie. "Marcus and Mildred" dine at the Colony and make "polite whoopee." Another series is entitled *Collectors, Average and Mean* and includes figures that contemplate gold, nudes, and cacti in a Cubist style. *A Summer Afternoon at Coney Island: Native Fauna Observed by Covarrubias* depicts the crowds at Coney Island. Covarrubias' images are not drawn with scientific precision. Rather, they are caricatures that exaggerate physical form and behavior. *Vanity Fair*, multiple issues from the 1920s, no dates listed, Covarrubias Papers, Folder 567.
40. Frank Crowninshield, Introduction, in Miguel Covarrubias, *Negro Drawings* (New York: Knopf, 1927), no page numbers.
41. Walter Pach wrote in a review when the book came out: "The range in the drawings is a wide one; they go from broad burlesque, through sensuality, through hysterical religiosity, worldliness, vice and sheer animal spirits to a

few, but all-important gestures of nobility." (Pach, "An Artist Looks on Harlem," November 6, 1927.) A reviewer from the *Greensboro Record* (Greensboro, N.C.) wrote, "It is useless . . . to label him caricaturist or cartoonist, cubist or impressionist." Edwin Bjorkman, "Three Artists," *Greensboro Record,* no date, Covarrubias Papers, Folder 426.

42. Countee Cullen, "The Dark Tower," *Opportunity,* 6, no. 2 (February 1928), quoted in Williams, *Covarrubias,* 48.

43. Covarrubias, quoted in Marcel Haldeman-Julius, "Miguel Covarrubias: A Brilliant Mexican Youth Who Has Won the Plaudits of American Notables," undated pamphlet, Covarrubias Papers, Folder 426.

44. Bjorkman, "Three Artists."

45. Crowninshield, Introduction.

46. Pach wrote that Covarrubias could "make the dark happy people live before us . . . [and saw] them with an eye of such deep understanding" because "in the land where he was born, primitive passion, religiosity and heroism are to be found on the streets of the modern Capital side-by-side with the most recent products of invention and culture. And so it was natural for Covarrubias to succeed in portraying the men and women who evolved the cake-walk—and the spirituals." Walter Pach, "An Artist Looks on Harlem."

47. Critic John Selby of the *Literary Guidepost* wrote, "It seemed to [Miguel] that Bali was one of the few remaining graces still in existence, possessing the best elements of civilization lost to the mechanized Western worlds—a world which for him had taken on many aspects of Eliot's 'Waste Land.'" John Selby, review of *Island of Bali,* in *Literary Guidepost,* unidentified, undated newspaper, quoted in Williams, *Covarrubias,* 62.

48. In fact, when Covarrubias and his wife returned from one of their year-long stays there (in 1934), one of the first visits he made in New York was to Mason, who was in New York Hospital at the time. Williams, *Covarrubias,* 80.

49. Covarrubias received very positive reviews, which, according to his biographer Adriana Williams, lauded him for "his interest in everyday life, his historical-anthropological perspective with which he interpreted everyday life, his extraordinary knowledge of ethnic people, art, and culture, and his ability and facility to make researcher and aesthete compatible." This approbation resonates with Hurston's methods, for she too employed the aesthetic and the anthropological. (Williams, *Covarrubias,* 83–84.) A Wisconsin newspaper published a review that declared, "Only through the sympathetic eyes of an artist could he have penetrated so deeply into the spirit of the dance, theatre, music, handicraft and sports of Bali; and only a man of learning in anthropology could have understood and recorded its religion, family life and economic and political organization," (*Waukesha Freeman* [Waukesha, Wisconsin], January 15, 1938, reprinted in Williams, *Covarrubias,* 83.) It is significant that this review describes Covarrubias' ability to "penetrate" the culture of Bali. Boas used this word to describe Hurston's efforts.

50. Zora Neale Hurston to Miguel Covarrubias, January 31, 1935, and May 21,

1935, Covarrubias Papers, Folder 195,. Although Hurston refers to the list of illustrations, I was unable to locate them among Covarrubias' papers.

51. Hurston, *Mules and Men,* 139.

52. Ibid., 141–142.

53. Ibid., 43.

54. Elaine Scarry, *Dreaming by the Book* (Princeton: Princeton University Press, 1999), 6.

55. Hurston, *Mules and Men,* 43.

56. Covarrubias' sketch bears the mark of erasing, suggesting that he was working on how to represent formally the physical experience of praying. Covarrubias Papers Folder 119.

57. Hurston, *Mules and Men,* 86–88.

58. Miguel Covarrubias, *Island of Bali* (New York: Knopf, 1956), between 226 and 227.

59. Mark Twain, *Pudd'nhead Wilson* (Hartford, Conn.: American Publishing, 1899), 9.

60. For an exploration of the visual and literary depictions of Roxy, see Werner Sollors, "Was Roxy Black?" in Jonathan Brennan, ed., *Mixed Race Literature* (Stanford: Stanford University Press, 2002), 74.

61. Hurston, *Mules and Men,* 247.

5. Realistic Tongues

1. Sterling Brown, *The Negro in American Fiction* (New York: Atheneum, 1969), 1–2.

2. Ibid., 3.

3. Ibid., 4.

4. Ibid., 160–161. Alain Locke also saw "something too Arcadian" about *Mules and Men.* Alain Locke, "Deep River, Deeper Sea: Retrospective Review of the Literature of the Negro for 1935," *Opportunity,* 14 (January 1936), reprinted in Jeffrey Stewart, ed., *The Critical Temper of Alain Locke* (New York: Garland, 1983), 239.

5. See Miguel Covarrubias Papers, Universidad de las Americas, Puebla, Mexico, Folder 262.

6. When whites are mentioned in Hurston's account of Southern folk life, they damage the African American world not because they engage in lynching, Klan activity, or other forms of violence, but because they undermine the intraracial community. Hurston writes of Woodbridge, a nearby town: "It is a Negro community joining Maitland on the north as Eatonville does on the west, but no enterprising souls have ever organized it. They have no schoolhouse, no post office, no mayor. It is lacking in Eatonville's feeling of unity. In fact, a white woman lives there." Zora Neale Hurston, *Mules and Men* (Philadelphia: Lippincott, 1935), 29.

7. Anonymous, "Richard Wright's Powerful Narrative Beautifully Illustrated in

New Book," *Sunday Worker* (New York), November 9, 1941, in John M. Reilly, ed., *Richard Wright: The Critical Reception* (New York: Burt Franklin, 1978), 101.

8. Ernestine Rose, article in *Library Journal,* 66, November 15, 1941, ibid., 106.

9. Anonymous, "The March of the Negro," *New York World-Telegram,* November 11, 1941, ibid., 104.

10. Horace Cayton, "Wright's New Book More than a Study of Social Status," *Pittsburgh Courier,* November 15, 1941, ibid., 105. According to Michel Fabre, Cayton shared his research for *Black Metropolis* with Wright. Michel Fabre, *The Unfinished Quest of Richard Wright* (Chicago: University of Chicago Press, 1993).

11. Anonymous, "Richard Wright's Powerful Narrative Beautifully Illustrated in New Book," 101.

12. W. J. T. Mitchell, *Picture Theory* (Chicago: University of Chicago Press, 1994), 94.

13. Ibid., 281.

14. The term is John Puckett's. See John Rogers Puckett, *Five Photo-Textual Documentaries from the Great Depression* (Ann Arbor: UMI Research Press, 1984).

15. Archibald MacLeish, *Land of the Free* (New York: Harcourt, Brace, 1938), 89. MacLeish selected the photographs and wrote the accompanying poem.

16. Other books included Herman Clarence Nixon's *Forty Acres and Steel Mules* (1938), Samuel Chamberlain's *Fair Is Our Land* (1942), Jack Delano and Arthur Raper's *Tenants of the Almighty* (1943), and James Agee and Walker Evans' *Let Us Now Praise Famous Men* (1941).

17. William Stott, *Documentary Expression and Thirties America* (New York: Oxford University Press, 1973), 71–72.

18. Laura Wexler, *Tender Violence: Domestic Visions in an Age of U.S. Imperialism* (Chapel Hill: University of North Carolina Press, 2000), 4.

19. Alain Locke, "The Saving Grace of Realism: A Retrospective Review of the Literature of the Negro for 1933," *Opportunity,* 13 (January 1934), reprinted in Cary Wintz, ed., *The Critics and the Harlem Renaissance* (New York: Garland, 1996), 272.

20. Alain Locke, "This Year of Grace: Outstanding Books of the Year in Negro Literature," *Opportunity,* 9 (February 1931), reprinted ibid., 257.

21. Locke, "The Saving Grace of Realism," 272.

22. Locke observed the rise of realism from the early 1930s. In his retrospective review of the literature of 1931, he wrote that "the outlines of the Negro projected by the cold November sun of our day are realistically sharp and clear." He continued, "All the minds preoccupied today with the Negro are truth-seeking, even those who do not find it, and more serious revision of the old views and notions has come from the press this year than could have been wildly dreamed of or was ever demanded by those who chafed and smarted under what they called the 'conspiracy of misrepresentation.' Northern and

Southern, Negro and white alike, have come to closer realistic grips with
present fact and historical situation and record, and if truth can lead us to
higher beauty, the prospect is hopeful." Alain Locke, "We Turn to Prose: A
Retrospective Review of the Literature of the Negro for 1931," *Opportunity*,
10 (February 1932), reprinted in Wintz, *The Critics and the Harlem Renaissance*, 260–261.

23. Alain Locke, "Jingo, Counter-Jingo, and Us: A Retrospective Review of the
Literature of the Negro for 1937," *Opportunity*, 17 (January 1938), reprinted ibid., 308.

24. Julia Peterkin, *Roll, Jordan, Roll* (New York: R. O. Ballou, 1933), 9.

25. Nicholas Natanson, *The Black Image in the New Deal: The Politics of FSA
Photography* (Knoxville: University of Tennessee Press, 1992), 215.

26. Ibid., 4.

27. David Bradley, introduction to Wright, *Twelve Million Black Voices* (New
York: Thunder's Mouth Press, 1988), iv.

28. Elizabeth McCausland, "Photographic Books," in Willard D. Morgan, ed.,
The Encyclopedia of Photography (New York: National Educational Alli-
ance, 1949), 2794.

29. Natanson, *The Black Image in the New Deal*, 244–245.

30. In fact, one review juxtaposes *Twelve Million Black Voices* with other photo-
text combinations. John Field Mulholland wrote, "In an era of pictorial magazines, books which are primarily pictorial are to be expected, so only a book
of exceptional photographic excellence needs mention. . . . Pictures and
text are so interwoven as to make a book of unusual appeal." John Field
Mulholland, "Negroes in Pictures and Text," *Christian Century*, 50 (February 18, 1942), in Reilly, *Richard Wright: The Critical Reception*, 115.

31. Despite its differences in content from other photo-texts of the era, *Twelve
Million Black Voices* is similar to them in form and, in fact, almost identical to Sherwood Anderson's *Home Town*. One hundred forty-seven images,
most from the FSA, accompany the text, which nonetheless dominates the
volume. The images are by a number of FSA photographers and were culled
from various collections within the Historical Section of the FSA.

32. Richard Wright, *Twelve Million Black Voices* (New York: Viking, 1941), 10

33. Ibid., 11.

34. Ibid., 43.

35. The rhetoric of strangeness and the direct address to the white reader are very
similar to the language W. E. B. Du Bois uses in *The Souls of Black Folk*.
Moreover, Wright's declaration about historical perspective—"Standing now
at the apex of the twentieth century, we look back over the road we have
traveled and compare it with the road over which the white folks have traveled, and we see that three hundred years in the history of our lives are equivalent to two thousand years in the history of the lives of whites!"—is a reference to Du Bois's statement about the color line. Du Bois writes, "Herein lie
buried many things which if read with patience may show the strange meaning of being black here at the dawning of the Twentieth Century. The mean-

ing is not without interest to you, Gentle Reader; for the problem of the Twentieth Century is the problem of the color line." Wright, *Twelve Million Black Voices,* 145; W. E. B. Du Bois, *The Souls of Black Folk* (New York: Signet, 1982), xi.

36. Wright, *Twelve Million Black Voices,* 145.
37. Ibid., 35.
38. In fact, one critic adopted this metaphor of painting and described "the compelling word pictures [Wright] paints." Anonymous, "Richard Wright's Powerful Narrative Beautifully Illustrated in New Book," 102.
39. Wright, *Twelve Million Black Voices,* 40.
40. Ibid., xx.
41. Ibid., 16.
42. Ibid., 14.
43. Du Bois, in *The Souls of Black Folk,* uses some of the same rhetoric. He writes of "the shimmering swirl of waters where many, many thoughts ago the slave-ship first saw the square of Jamestown" (121).
44. Wright, *Twelve Million Black Voices,* 35.
45. Ibid., 41.
46. Ibid.
47. Ibid., 104.
48. Ibid., 105–106.
49. Ibid., 147.
50. Ibid., 31.
51. Ibid., 101.
52. Ibid., 51.
53. Ibid., 49.
54. Paul Valéry, "The Centenary of Photography," *Occasions,* in Alan Trachtenberg, ed., *Classic Essays on Photography* (New Haven, Conn.: Leete's Island Books, 1980), 195.
55. Lawrence Levine, "The Historian and the Icon," in Carl Fleischauer and Beverly Brennan, eds., *Documenting America, 1935–1943* (Berkeley: University of California Press, 1988), 23.
56. In the reprint published by Thunder's Mouth Press in 1988, the photograph by Richard Wright has been replaced by one from the U.S. Office of War Information. The image is not as powerful as Wright's. It shows an outhouse that bears a "For Colored" sign, but it does not highlight the written word.
57. Wright, *Twelve Million Black Voices,* 112.
58. Ibid., 17–18.
59. Mitchell, *Picture Theory,* 281–283.
60. The final page, however, includes three paragraphs about the kitchenette.
61. Alan Trachtenberg, *Reading American Photographs* (New York: Hill and Wang, 1989), xv.
62. Natanson, *The Black Image in the New Deal,* 251.
63. Wright, *Twelve Million Black Voices,* 49.

64. James Agee and Walker Evans, *Let Us Now Praise Famous Men* (Boston: Houghton Mifflin, 1939; rpt. 1988), 436–437.

65. Wright, *Twelve Million Black Voices,* 41.

66. Wright states, "The land we till is beautiful, with red and black and brown clay, with fresh and hungry smells, with pine trees and palm trees, with rolling hills and swampy delta—an unbelievably fertile land." Wright, *Twelve Million Black Voices,* 32.

67. Ibid., 43.

68. Cayton, "Wright's New Book More than a Study of Social Status," 105.

69. Wright, *Twelve Million Black Voices,* 69–70.

6. Silhouettes

1. See, for example, Robert O'Brien Hokanson, "Jazzing It Up: The Be-Bop Modernism of Langston Hughes," *Mosaic: A Journal for the Interdisciplinary Study of Literature,* 31, no. 4 (1994); David Chinitz, "Literacy and Authenticity: The Blues Poems of Langston Hughes," *Callaloo: A Journal of African-American and African Arts and Letters,* 19, no. 1 (Winter 1996); Nicholas M. Evans, "Langston Hughes as Bop Ethnographer in 'Trumpet Player: 52nd Street,'" *Library Chronicle of the University of Texas,* 24, nos. 1–2 (1994); Patricia E. Bonner, "Cryin' the Jazzy Blues and Livin' Blue Jazz: Analyzing the Blues and Jazz Poetry of Langston Hughes," *West Georgia College Review,* 20 (May 1990); and Richard K. Barksdale, "Langston Hughes and the Blues He Couldn't Lose," in Amritjit Singh, William S. Shiver, and Brodwin Stanley, eds., *The Harlem Renaissance: Revaluations* (New York: Garland, 1989).

2. Langston Hughes, "Montage of a Dream Deferred," in Arnold Rampersad, ed., *The Collected Poems of Langston Hughes* (New York: Knopf, 1994), 387.

3. These were *The Dream Keeper* (1932), illustrated by Helen Sewell; *The Negro Mother* (1932) and *Scottsboro Limited* (1932), illustrated by Prentiss Taylor; *Shakespeare in Harlem* (1942), illustrated by E. McKnight Kauffer; and *One-Way Ticket* (1949), illustrated by Jacob Lawrence. In addition, Hughes published *The Sweet Flypaper of Life* (1955), with photographs by Roy DeCarava; *A Pictorial History of the Negro in America* (1956); and a children's book, *Popo and Fifina,* illustrated by E. Simms Campbell.

4. Langston Hughes to Blanche Knopf, September 18, 1947, Langston Hughes Papers, Collection of American Literature, Beinecke Rare Book and Manuscript Library, Yale University.

5. Jacob Lawrence to Langston Hughes, September 28, 1947, Hughes Papers. Lawrence wrote, "Dear Mr. Hughes, Received your manuscript and also your letter. If all works out satisfactory with our agents, I know I will enjoy working on your book as our subject matter is similar."

6. Arnold Rampersad, *The Life of Langston Hughes,* Vol. 2, *1941–1967: I Dream a World* (New York: Oxford University Press, 1988), 153.

7. *One-Way Ticket* contains six drawings, all of which are linked to poems. Lawrence's drawing *Silhouette* accompanies the poems "Flight" and "Silhouette." "The Ballad of Margie Polite" is the title of both a poem and drawing, as are the phrases "One-Way Ticket" and "Graduation." The drawing *Too Blue* refers to a section and poem that bear the name "Too Blue." The drawing *Home in a Box* illustrates an entire section, although the title of the drawing is a paraphrase of the poem "Deceased." This chapter will explore "Flight," "Silhouette," "The Ballad of Margie Polite," "One-Way Ticket," "Too Blue," and "Home in a Box." "Graduation" operates like "Too Blue."

8. Tolson wrote, "*One-Way Ticket* shows that he is still the sophisticate and humanist on Vine Street, Lenox Avenue, Rampart Street, Beale Street, South Parkway, South Street, Elm Street, Texas Avenue, and Central Avenue. Langston Hughes is the poet of the urban Negro as Paul Laurence Dunbar was the poet of the rural Negro." M. B. Tolson, "Books and Authors: Let My People Go," *Southwestern Journal,* 4 (Fall–Winter 1948), 41–43, in Tish Dace, *Langston Hughes: The Contemporary Reviews* (New York: Cambridge University Press, 1997), 323. A review in the *Virginia Kirkus Bulletin* asserted that *One-Way Ticket* was "not quite a satisfactory mixture either as pure poetry or human appeal." Anonymous, "The Poetry of the Negro: *One-Way Ticket,*" *Virginia Kirkus Bulletin,* 16 (November 15, 1948), ibid., 324. The *Pittsburgh Courier* published a review that declared, "Indeed, a number of ordinary Negro lyric writers have ground out better stuff between drinks—and are still doing so." G. R. Cameron, "Langston Hughes Is Overrated as No. 1, Critic Claims," *Pittsburgh Courier,* 5 (February 1949), ibid., 336.

9. Alain Locke, "Wisdom *de Profundis:* The Literature of the Negro, 1949," *Phylon,* 11 (January–March 1950), reprinted in Jeffrey Stewart, *The Critical Temper of Alain Locke* (New York: Garland, 1983), 357.

10. J. Saunders Redding, review of *One-Way Ticket,* in *Saturday Review,* January 22, 1949, in Henry Louis Gates and K. A. Appiah, eds., *Langston Hughes: Critical Perspectives, Past and Present* (New York: Amistad, 1993), 31.

11. Ibid.

12. Ellen Harkins Wheat, *Jacob Lawrence, American Painter* (Seattle: University of Washington Press, 1986), 42.

13. August Derleth in fact used the same language as Hughes. He wrote, "This new book has all of the virtues of its predecessor, and in addition it has striking illustrations by Jacob Lawrence, admirably complementary to the text." August Derleth, "The New Poetry," *Capital Times,* January 16, 1949, in Dace, *Langston Hughes,* 331.

14. Gladys P. Graham, "Books on Review: A Poet Speaks Out for Black Americans," *New Jersey Herald News* (January or February 1949), ibid., 324.

15. Rudolph Aggrey, "Hughes' New Book *One-Way Ticket* Offers Frank, Humor-Spiked Verse," *Cleveland Call and Post,* January 1, 1949, ibid., 325.

16. Wheat, *Jacob Lawrence*, 29.
17. It is possible to see Lawrence's series as indicating a jealousy of literature's narrative potential, of a presumed ease of historical rendition in the textual. In *One-Way Ticket*, however, this jealousy is assuaged by the poems, which offer their own narration, although they do not function in the same straight-forward manner as the captions in Lawrence's own series.
18. See Deborah Willis, "The Schomburg Collection: A Rich Resource for Jacob Lawrence," in Elizabeth Hutton Turner, *Jacob Lawrence: The Migration Series* (Washington, D.C.: Rappahannock, 1993).
19. Lawrence to Hughes, May 5, 1948, Hughes Papers.
20. The drawings in *One-Way Ticket* follow or interrupt the poems they illustrate.
21. Langston Hughes, *One-Way Ticket* (New York: Knopf, 1949), 55.
22. Ibid., 56.
23. Wheat, *Jacob Lawrence*, 24.
24. Rampersad, *The Life of Langston Hughes*, Vol. 2, 75.
25. Hughes to Arna Bontemps, August 5, 1943, in Charles Nichols, ed., *Arna Bontemps–Langston Hughes: Letters, 1925–1967* (New York: Paragon, 1990), 135.
26. Hughes, *One-Way Ticket*, 75–78.
27. Ibid., 78.
28. Ibid., 61–62.
29. Lawrence's *Migration Series* contains a number of scenes meant to evoke the physical act of the migration itself. One panel in particular bears a striking resemblance to his black-and-white drawing. Panel 32 depicts one of many "railroad stations in the South [that] were crowded with people leaving for the North." The waiting migrants sit in rows on benches, with their backs to the viewer. These are undifferentiated individuals. They are all represented in the same colors (black and brown), with occasional variations of blue, yellow, red, and green, which depict hats and shirts. In the upper left-hand corner of the frame sits a young boy, dressed in white, with orange socks and hat. He sits on a piece of luggage and faces the waiting people. Almost as if he is onstage in front of an audience, he faces the viewer directly. In contrast to the figure in the drawing *One-Way Ticket*, he possesses no facial features. He is a representative of the moment of transition, even if he is different from the others.
30. Hughes, *One-Way Ticket*, 102.
31. Ibid.

Epilogue

1. Alain Locke, "The Negro: 'New' or Newer—A Retrospective Review of the Literature of the Negro for 1938," *Opportunity*, 17 (January–February 1939), reprinted in Jeffrey Stewart, *The Critical Temper of Alain Locke* (New York: Garland, 1983), 271.

2. Ibid.

3. Alain Locke Papers, Moorland-Spingarn Room, Howard University, Box 122, Folder 24.

4. Locke, "The Negro: 'New' or Newer," 273.

5. Ibid., 279.

6. Alain Locke, Wisdom *de Profundis:* The Literature of the Negro, 1949," *Phylon,* 11 (January–June 1950), reprinted in Stewart, *The Critical Temper of Alain Locke,* 357.

7. Alain Locke, "Who and What Is 'Negro'?" *Opportunity,* 20 (February–March 1942), reprinted in Stewart, *The Critical Temper of Alain Locke,* 310.

8. Ibid.

9. Alain Locke, "Up Till Now," *The Negro Artist Comes of Age: A National Survey of Contemporary American Artists* (Albany Institute of History and Art Exhibition of January 3–February 11, 1945), reprinted in Stewart, *The Critical Temper of Alain Locke,* 192.

10. Ibid., 193.

11. Ibid., 194.

12. Alain Locke, "Advance on the Art Front," *Opportunity,* 17 (January–February 1939), reprinted in Stewart, *The Critical Temper of Alain Locke,* 186.

13. Ibid., 188.

14. Locke, "Who and What Is 'Negro'?" 309.

Index